THE BOARDROOM CISO

ANTONIO BOVOSO

THE BOARDROOM CISO

THE ART OF TRANSLATING CYBER RISK

CONSIRO PRESS

This book is provided for general informational and educational purposes only. It does not constitute legal, regulatory, cybersecurity, privacy, financial, or other professional advice.

The information and opinions expressed herein reflect the author's experience and research at the time of writing, but may not reflect the most current legal developments, regulatory guidance, or security practices. Cybersecurity, privacy, and artificial intelligence risk management are complex, rapidly evolving fields, and no publication can address all circumstances or provide definitive guidance for every organization.

Readers should not act or refrain from acting based solely on the content of this book without seeking appropriate professional advice tailored to their specific situation. The author and publisher expressly disclaim any liability for any loss, damage, or disruption arising from the use of, or reliance upon, the information contained in this book. This book is not intended to create, and does not create, any advisor-client, attorney-client, or fiduciary relationship.

References to artificial intelligence systems, tools, and governance frameworks are illustrative and do not constitute endorsements, warranties, or guarantees of performance, security, or regulatory compliance.

CONSIRO PRESS
Boston, MA
www.consiro.io/press

Cover Design by Mersina Designs
Layout Design by Mersina Designs
Developmental Editor: Gabriella Williams
Library of Congress Control Number: 2026904191
Copy Editor: Liz Wheeler
Hardcover ISBN: 979-8-9946435-0-1
Paperback ISBN: 979-8-9946435-1-8
First edition

To my loving family

Introduction

The boardroom is where strategy meets scrutiny, and nowhere is this more evident than in cybersecurity. For too long, the conversation has been a monologue: security leaders speaking a language of threats, vulnerabilities, and technical controls, while board members listen in a dialect of revenue, risk, and regulation. The result is a chasm of understanding, a gap between what is said and what is heard.

This book is about bridging that gap. It is about the *art of translation*: transforming complex cybersecurity realities into clear, actionable business insights for the board. It is about moving beyond technical jargon to speak the language of enterprise value, exposure, and strategy.

My journey to this understanding was not linear. Like many cyber executives, I started my career deeply immersed in the technical trenches. My early board presentations were often a flurry of charts, metrics, and dire warnings, delivered with the earnest belief that more data equaled more understanding. I learned the hard way that it did not. The board did not need more information; they needed more insight. They did not need a technical deep dive; they needed a strategic compass. That realization changed everything. I stopped seeing my role as merely a guardian of systems and began to embrace it as an architect of resilience and a designer of confidence. My job became less about explaining all the operational tasks we accomplished and more about articulating why a specific control matters to the company's bottom line, its market position, or its ability to innovate.

This book is the culmination of those lessons. It is a practical guide for cybersecurity and technology executives who need to communicate effectively with the board of directors and non-technical executives.

After reading it, you'll know how to do several things:

Understand the board's perspective
: Learn what truly motivates board members, their fiduciary duties, and their primary concerns.

Translate cyber risk into business language
: Develop frameworks to articulate threats, vulnerabilities, and incidents in terms of enterprise value, exposure, and strategic impact.

Build effective governance frameworks
: Design and present governance structures that resonate with board expectations and regulatory requirements.

Present metrics that matter
: Select and communicate key performance indicators that provide meaningful insight into the security posture, focusing on exposure, resilience, and assurance.

Master boardroom presentations
: Craft compelling narratives, manage Q&A sessions, and project executive presence.

Navigate crisis communications
: Lead with composure during incidents, providing clear, predictable updates that build trust rather than erode it.

Align cybersecurity with business strategy
Integrate security initiatives directly into corporate objectives, demonstrating how protection enables growth and innovation.

Each chapter offers practical advice and real-world examples. This is not a theoretical thesis; it is a field guide, born from years in the boardroom trenches. It is about turning the often-abstract world of cybersecurity into a tangible, strategic asset for your organization.

The goal is simple: to empower you to move beyond being a technical expert to becoming a trusted strategic partner. When you master the art of translation, you do not just protect the company; you help shape its future.

Why This Book, and Why Now

Cybersecurity now influences everything:

- Revenue
- Reputation
- Investor confidence
- Corporate strategy
- Operational resilience
- And much more

Yet many chief information security officers struggle not because they lack capability, but because they lack translation. The boardroom has become their new command center, and no one teaches the language.

This book fills that gap.

How to Use This Book

There are several ways to approach this book. I will describe how I intended it to be used, but as you will see in my writing, I want you to apply it in a way that works for your style and your environment.

First, read the book straight through. This will give you a comprehensive view of the boardroom landscape, the skills needed to influence, and the tools to communicate at the board level.

If you are preparing for a board meeting in the next few days, read the What to Carry Forward sections at the end of each chapter, which will help you manage your message in the meeting.

Finally, use the tools in the appendices when you are preparing critical updates. You will find the following:

- Quick reference checklists with countdown steps to prepare for the board update
- Translation of standard cyber terms in language aligned to board responsibilities
- Additional reading and websites that can support your development

A Note on Scenarios

The scenarios in this book are drawn from my career experience and lessons learned from colleagues. Details and names have been changed to protect confidentiality, and some examples are composites that reflect common patterns I have observed across multiple industries. Whether a scenario is a direct account or a composite, the dynamics, mistakes, and behaviors all apply to the real world.

PART I

The Strategic Foundation

"If one does not know to which port one is sailing, no wind is favorable."

— Seneca

Chapter 1

Understanding the Board's Perspective

The audit chair just asked you a direct question: "Who on this board is accountable if we have a material breach?"

You start to answer, then stop. Is she asking about legal liability? Oversight responsibility? Reputational risk?

The CFO jumps in. "I think she's asking about fiduciary duty and whether we've met our standard of care."

You nod, as you know the terms, but not exactly how they apply to your message about controls and frameworks. You know less about what keeps directors up at night and why they're personally exposed when cyber risk isn't managed well.

The audit chair is still waiting for your answer.

You cannot influence a board conversation until you understand who you are speaking to and what lens they use to evaluate risk, value, and leadership. This chapter walks you through the board's world: their duties, and what matters to them when you present.

Board Fundamentals: Purpose and Fiduciary Duties

The board exists to represent shareholders and stakeholders. Its function is oversight, not operational management. Their job is to ensure governance is effective.

Directors are personally accountable for the organization's integrity, sustainability, and strategic direction. That accountability creates pressure you might not see from your seat. When directors ask questions, they are not testing your technical knowledge. They are confirming that you understand the business consequences and can assist them in fulfilling their legal obligations.

Three Core Fiduciary Duties for Boards

Every board operates under three legal responsibilities—duty of care, duty of loyalty, and duty of oversight:

Duty of care

Directors must review materials, ask questions, seek expert input, and act with reasonable diligence. When you present to the board, you help them fulfill this duty. If your update is vague or incomplete, you are putting them at risk.

Duty of loyalty

Directors must act in the organization's best interest, not their own. They avoid conflicts of interest and maintain confidentiality. This is why boards are sensitive to disclosure, insider information, and anything that could create legal exposure.

Duty of oversight

Directors must ensure the organization has adequate controls and monitoring, including cybersecurity. Since the Security and Exchange Commission's (SEC) 2023 cybersecurity disclosure rules, boards are explicitly accountable for cyber risk oversight.

Put simply, boards are required by regulators to address cyber risk. Your job is to give them what they need to govern responsibly.

What This Means for CISOs

Directors depend on you for trustworthy information. They cannot oversee what they don't understand. That is why clarity matters more than technical depth.

When you contextualize risk in business terms, such as exposure to revenue, reputation, and regulatory penalties, you help the board fulfill its fiduciary duty.

How Boards Review Materials

Boards do not operate like executive teams. Their role is to evaluate, challenge, and advise on management's direction. Understanding their process helps you position your messaging effectively.

The Board Review Cycle

Most boards follow a deliberate path:

Pre-reads

Materials go out days before the meeting. Directors review them in advance. Many have thoughts on direction before the meeting even starts. If your pre-read is unclear, you have already lost momentum.

Committee review

Major topics are routed through committees first. The audit committee reviews financial controls and compliance. The risk committee examines enterprise risk appetite. The technology committee evaluates digital strategy. Committees vet topics, ask hard questions, and make recommendations to the full board.

Executive alignment

Before the board weighs in, the CEO, CFO, and other executives align. Directors watch for inconsistencies between leaders. If the CISO and CFO tell different stories about cyber investment, the board might defer approval until they can get a clear message.

Board discussion

The full board hears recommendations, asks clarifying questions, and tests assumptions. They are looking for blind spots, unintended consequences, and whether leadership has thought through second-order effects.

Vote or consensus

Some approvals (budget, CEO hiring, mergers and acquisitions [M&A] matters) require a formal vote. Other times, consensus is reached through discussion. Either way, directors are cautious. They move forward when they have confidence, not when they are rushed.

Given your organization's structure, your board update might only go to a committee, so it is critical that they understand your message, especially if they present it to the full board without you in the room.

What CISOs Should Do

Get your materials done early. Make pre-reads concise. Anticipate questions and prepare clear, candid answers. Boards respond well to leaders who respect their process and make it easy for them to govern.

Board Committee Structures and Roles

Each committee has a specific mandate. Understanding committee structures helps you tailor your message and know who to engage. See Figure 1.1 for an overview of important committees, their areas of focus, and how to engage them.

Audit Committee

The audit committee oversees financial reporting, internal controls, and regulatory compliance. In many organizations, cybersecurity sits here because it connects to financial risk and disclosure obligations.

Key responsibilities:

- Control effectiveness and assurance
- Financial impact of cyber incidents
- Compliance with regulations, such as SOX (Sarbanes-Oxley Act), SEC, GDPR (General Data Protection Regulation), and others
- Audit findings and remediation timelines
- Disclosure accuracy

How to engage them: Focus on control posture, compliance status, and financial exposure. Be ready to discuss audit results, gaps, and how you are closing them. The audit committee wants evidence that controls are in place and working.

Risk Committee

The risk committee evaluates enterprise-wide risk, including cyber, operational, strategic, and reputational risk. They set risk appetite and monitor whether the organization's exposure stays within tolerance.

Key responsibilities:

- Risk appetite and tolerance levels
- Emerging threats and trend analysis
- Risk mitigation strategies and trade-offs
- How cyber risk aligns with other enterprise risks
- Scenario planning and resilience

How to engage them: Frame cyber risk in enterprise terms. Show how it connects to strategic objectives, growth initiatives, and operational resilience. Risk committees appreciate scenario-based discussions: if this scenario occurs, here is the impact and here is our response.

Technology Committee

Not every board has a technology committee, but they are becoming more common. These committees focus on digital strategy, innovation, and technology enablement.

Key responsibilities:

- How technology supports business strategy
- Digital transformation and competitive advantage
- Technology investments and return on investment (ROI)
- Emerging technology risks and opportunities, such as AI and cloud transformation
- Talent and capability gaps

How to engage them: Position cybersecurity as an enabler of innovation and trust. Talk about how security supports digital initiatives, protects customer experience, and builds competitive differentiation. Technology committees are more receptive to discussions about architecture, emerging threats, and strategic investments.

Governance and Nominating Committee

This committee oversees board composition, director education, and governance practices. While they don't typically engage deeply with cyber topics, they often care about board education and whether directors have the expertise to oversee digital risk.

Key responsibilities:

- Board composition and expertise gaps
- Director education and training
- Governance policies and practices
- Succession planning

How to engage them: Offer board education sessions. Provide concise primers on emerging risks. Governance committees appreciate CISOs who help the board stay informed without overwhelming them.

Committee Coordination Matters

When you present to one committee, assume other committees will hear about it. Keep your message consistent across committees. If the audit committee hears one version of your budget request and the risk committee hears another, you create confusion and lose credibility.

Board Risk Evaluation Framework

Boards evaluate risk differently from operational leaders. Understanding their framework helps you position cyber risk in terms they recognize and can act on.

KNOW YOUR AUDIENCE: BOARD COMMITTEE FOCUS AREAS

AUDIT COMMITTEE

Focus Areas:
- Control effectiveness and assurance
- Financial impact of cyber incidents
- Compliance (SOX, SEC, GDPR)
- Audit findings and remediation
- Disclosure accuracy

Key Questions:
"Are controls working?"
"What did the auditors find?"

How to Engage:
Focus on control posture, compliance status, and financial exposure. Be ready to discuss audit results and gaps.

RISK COMMITTEE

Focus Areas:
- Risk appetite and tolerance levels
- Emerging threats and trend analysis
- Risk mitigation strategies
- Enterprise risk alignment
- Scenario planning and resilience

Key Questions:
"Are we within our risk appetite?"
"What scenarios concern you?"

How to Engage:
Frame cyber risk in enterprise terms. Use scenario-based discussions: "if this happens, here's the impact."

TECHNOLOGY COMMITTEE

Focus Areas:
- Digital strategy and competitive edge
- Technology investments and ROI
- Emerging tech risks (AI, cloud)
- Digital transformation progress
- Talent and capability gaps

Key Questions:
"Does this support our growth?"
"What's the competitive impact?"

How to Engage:
Position cybersecurity as an enabler of innovation and trust. Discuss how security supports digital initiatives.

GOVERNANCE COMMITTEE

Focus Areas:
- Board composition and expertise
- Director education and training
- Governance policies and practices
- Succession planning

Key Questions:
"Does the board have the right expertise to oversee digital risk?"

How to Engage:
Offer board education sessions. Provide concise primers on emerging risks without overwhelming.

Figure 1.1. Board committee focus areas

The Board's Risk Lens

Directors assess risk at the intersection of likelihood and consequence. They think in scenarios and outcomes.

When you present a risk, boards are asking questions like the following:

- Could this disrupt our operations? Would it take down critical systems, halt production, or prevent us from serving customers?
- Could this trigger financial loss? What is the potential cost of direct loss, legal liability, regulatory fines, and insurance impact?
- Could this create regulatory or legal exposure? Do we have disclosure obligations? Could we face enforcement action or shareholder litigation?
- Could this affect our strategic initiatives? Would it delay a product launch, complicate an acquisition, or create a competitive disadvantage?

Risk Appetite and Tolerance

Boards set risk appetite, the amount and type of risk the organization is willing to accept. Your job is to help them understand whether current exposure is within that appetite.

If cyber risk exceeds appetite, you need a plan to reduce it, or a recommendation for the board to formally accept higher risk. If risk is within appetite, say so. Boards appreciate clarity on both sides of the line.

Board Culture and Communication Norms

Every boardroom has its own culture. Some are formal and structured. Others are conversational and collaborative. Understanding the culture helps you calibrate your delivery and read the room. You'll typically learn your board's culture through observation over two to three meetings, but you can get early signals by talking with peers who've presented to them, asking your CEO about the board's preferred style, or observing how the CEO structures updates for the board.

Common Board Cultures

While each board is unique, there are several common types of cultures you might encounter:

Formal and process-driven
These boards follow strict agendas, rely heavily on pre-reads, and expect presentations to be brief and disciplined. Questions are reserved for the end. Deviation from the agenda is rare.

Collaborative and inquisitive
These boards ask questions throughout your presentation. They probe assumptions, explore scenarios, and engage in real-time discussion. You need to be adaptable and comfortable with interruptions.

Consensus-oriented
These boards avoid formal votes and prefer to reach agreement through discussion. They test ideas, surface objections, and work toward alignment. Silence often means the room is still forming a view.

Directive and decisive
These boards move quickly. They ask sharp questions and expect clear recommendations. You need to be confident, concise, and ready with answers.

Note: Your board may not align neatly with any of these types. Listen and learn.

What to Carry Forward

- Understanding the board's perspective can change how you lead. Directors are not looking for technical expertise. They are looking for strategic judgment, business acumen, and the ability to help them fulfill their fiduciary obligations.
- When you understand how boards operate, what they care about, and how they evaluate risk, you stop trying to impress them with your knowledge and start enabling them to govern. That shift is what transforms a technical leader into a strategic advisor.
- The strongest CISOs make the board's job easier. They deliver clarity, not complexity, surface risk early, frame it in business terms, and provide clear recommendations. It is critical to respect the board's process, understand committee mandates, and align with other executives before the meeting.
- Your mission is not to showcase cybersecurity. It is to help the board protect the organization's future. When you do that well, you become indispensable.

Chapter 2

The Boardroom Imperative

You are sitting across from the audit committee. The CFO just wrapped her update. Now it is your turn. The schedule is running behind; you now have eight minutes for your report. Maybe you have to recommend that the company invest another $2 million in security controls; maybe you have to explain why last quarter's phishing incident will not become this quarter's regulatory fine.

The directors are attentive. They are not just listening; they are watching. How you frame cyber risk in the next few minutes will shape their confidence in your leadership for months to come.

The Boardroom Has Become Your Second Command Center

As recently as five to ten years ago, most CISOs presented to the board once a year, if at all. The update was ceremonial. Directors nodded, asked a few questions, and moved on.

That world is gone.

Today, cybersecurity commonly sits on the board agenda every quarter, sometimes every month, depending on circumstances. The Securities and Exchange Commission now requires public companies to disclose material cyber incidents within four business days, which allows investors to more easily scrutinize digital risk during earnings calls.

Put simply, cyber risk is now enterprise risk. Your relationship with the board is no longer optional. It is a foundational aspect of your role.

What This Means for You

If you lack the skill to explain cyber risk in business terms, you will struggle to influence how the board views your function. It snowballs from there. If you cannot shape the board's view of risk, you will struggle to secure the budget, authority, and executive support your program needs to succeed.

The boardroom is where your program can gain strategic momentum.

The Cost of the Gap

The shift from ceremonial board updates to quarterly cyber oversight was not gradual. It was driven by breaches at organizations like Equifax, SolarWinds, and Colonial Pipeline that exposed a governance gap most boards did not know they had: security tools generated alerts, but there was no clear escalation path to translate that technical data into board-level action. The governance structures that those organizations built after their respective crises are now baseline expectations. The modern board assumes its CISO can translate technical risk into business language, provide regular reporting, define clear escalation criteria, and connect metrics to fiduciary duty.

Your Role Has Shifted, and So Have the Rules

Many CISOs built their careers on technical mastery. They learned to architect defenses, hunt threats, and respond to incidents. That expertise still matters; it is now just part of the story.

The modern CISO operates at two altitudes:

- Operational: You manage controls, tools, and teams.
- Strategic: You translate technical reality into business enhancements and consequences.

Most CISOs are comfortable at the operational level. The strategic level, where you explain why a control gap threatens revenue or how vendor concentration creates acquisition risk, represents a significant shift in the story of risk. It requires a different vocabulary, a different tempo, and a different mindset.

In practice, this means that directors do not want to hear about your cloud access security broker (CASB) rules. They want to know whether customer data is protected, but care less about how many vulnerabilities you patched. They do care whether you are reducing exposure faster than threats are evolving, which is very hard to achieve, and whether you are confident the company can withstand the next SolarWinds-style supply chain attack. (They read the news.)

The shift from operator to advisor can be uncomfortable for some, but it is entirely possible and rewarding. Instead of operating alongside the business, you are integrated into the company's core strategy.

Consider the Board's Two Lenses

Before you present anything, understand this: most directors evaluate issues through two lenses: fiduciary and strategic. Miss either one, and your message may struggle to land. See Figure 2.1 for an overview of the two perspectives.

THE BOARD'S TWO LENSES

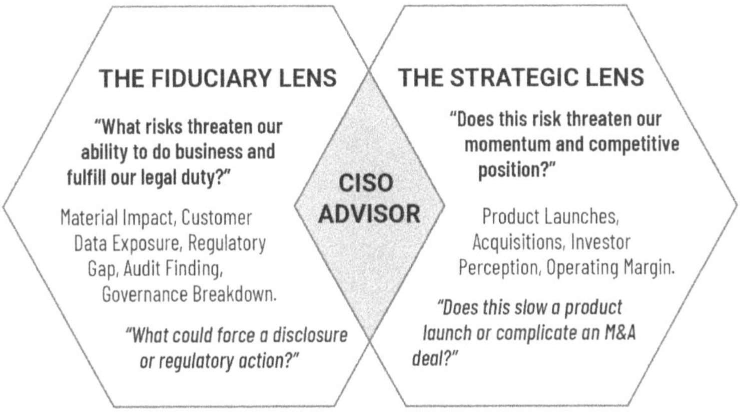

Figure 2.1. The board's two lenses

Lens 1: The Fiduciary Lens

Directors have a legal duty to protect the organization. They need to assess the following things:

- What risks threaten our ability to do business?
- What could force disclosure or regulatory action?
- Where are we exposed beyond our stated risk appetite?
- What would happen if this issue became public?

Certain words immediately trigger fiduciary concern: material impact, customer data exposure, regulatory gap, audit finding, and governance breakdown.

Lens 2: The Strategic Lens

Directors also care about momentum. They are concerned with the following:

- Does this risk slow a product launch?
- Does it complicate an acquisition or partnership?
- Does it change how investors or customers perceive us?
- Does it affect our competitive position or operating margin?

If you speak only in technical language, directors will try to interpret the strategic impact on their own. Often, they will get it wrong. Your job is to close that gap.

Do not say, "We have 200 critical vulnerabilities in our external attack surface." Instead, say, "We have identified exposure in three customer-facing systems. If exploited, this could disrupt order processing and trigger breach notification to 50,000 customers. We are prioritizing remediation by revenue impact."

One statement is a metric. The other is a business risk.

Reading the Room: What Directors Signal Without Speaking

Directors communicate long before they ask questions. If you learn to read body language and pacing, you will know whether your message is working in time to adjust.

Table 2.1 shows what to watch for.

Table 2.1. Reading the Room

Signal	What It Likely Means	How to Respond
Leaning forward	Rising concern or need for clarity	Slow down. Simplify your next point. Offer a concrete example.
Leaning back, touching head	Cognitive overload	Pause. Summarize what you just said in one sentence.

Signal	What It Likely Means	How to Respond
Sudden notetaking	You triggered something, good or bad	Note the topic. Expect a question. Be ready to expand or defend.
Side glances between directors	Shared doubt or forming objection	Pause and ask if there are any questions. If you can address the concern directly, do so; if you need some time to consider the question or objection, let them know that you are noting it and provide a timeline for when they can expect a response.

You are not mind-reading. You are interpreting real-time feedback. Adjust your narrative, not your facts.

What Boards Actually Care About

Remember, boards are concerned with the big picture: their primary responsibility is to make sure that the organization stays true to its mission and core values, and that the business is being run well. When it comes to cybersecurity, here are some examples of things the board is concerned with:

- Whether a cyber incident could force a financial restatement
- Whether your controls will satisfy the next System and Organization Controls (SOC) 2 audit
- Whether you are confident that the company can operate through a ransomware attack

- Whether you have stress-tested your incident response plan in the last 12 months

- Whether your third-party risk program covers vendors critical to company success

Put another way: directors care about outcomes, confidence, and evidence, not activity.

Directors gravitate toward paths that reduce uncertainty. If your framing adds uncertainty because it is too technical, too vague, or too contradictory, the room will shift away from you, or toward you in a way that can catch you off guard.

Who Is in the Room: A Quick Guide to the Board Roles Most Relevant to You

Depending on their roles, board directors have different priorities, different expertise, and different tolerances for risk.

In your role as a CISO, you will typically be most concerned with the following formal roles:

- **Board chair:** Sets the meeting tone and flow. Often the most influential voice.
- **Audit committee chair:** Your most likely ally for cyber oversight. Usually asks the sharpest questions.
- **Independent directors:** Bring outside perspective. Often challenge assumptions others accept.
- **Management directors:** Usually, the CEO and CFO. They bridge operational and strategic priorities.

The Board Member Types

Understanding roles is essential, but boards are composed of people, not organizational charts. When you enter the room, you will encounter a range of engagement levels. Not every director will be equally attentive or invested in your update.

The Engaged Director

When I first began my career, I thought all board members would fall into this category. They read every word of the pre-read, make eye contact, and you can see they have questions ready for you. Give them depth when requested; they will appreciate nuance, and their questions often help clarify your message for the rest of the room.

The Disengaged Director

I couldn't have been more shocked to see this person. Not paying attention, on their phone, almost as though they were there for a paycheck and to move on. (Be careful not to confuse them with the Quiet Genius, described next.)

Don't take it personally or try to win them over mid-presentation—focus on the directors who are engaged.

The Quiet Genius

In most of my meetings, there is one person who says little; they're paying attention, but, given their silence and lack of expression, you do not expect a question. Just when you've put them in the "disengaged" category, they ask you a question that shows they are not only listening, but have done their research.

Never assume silence means disinterest. Prepare for substantive questions and treat their inquiries as opportunities to demonstrate command of the details.

The Confrontational Director

This director treats your update as a stress test. They interrupt with sharp questions, challenge your data, and seem determined to find gaps in your logic.

Stay calm, acknowledge valid concerns directly, and don't get defensive. Composure under pressure often earns their respect more than perfect answers.

The Wild Card

There is often a director whom you can assign to any category. Over four quarters, you may find they fit into all these categories depending on the day, the meeting, or the topic.

Read the room in real time and adapt your approach; what worked last quarter may not work today, so stay flexible and responsive to their energy.

Each of these formal roles and character types requires a slightly different approach. Learn who these people are. Read about their backgrounds. Understand what they have publicly written, where they have worked, and what issues they prioritize.

This homework will save you in the room.

When Board Dynamics Become Dysfunctional

The preceding sections describe how to work with functional boards—even challenging ones. But not every board operates with the discipline, professionalism, or rationality you would expect. Some board cultures are fundamentally broken, and no amount of preparation, translation skill, or executive presence will fix them.

Recognizing dysfunctional board dynamics early is critical. These situations rarely improve on their own, and they can derail careers, damage reputations, and waste years of your professional life. Your responsibility is to repair broken relationships where possible, but also to recognize when a board culture is toxic and extraction is the right strategic move.

The Micromanaging Board

Some boards cannot distinguish between oversight and management. They question every tactical decision, second-guess operational choices, and demand involvement in matters that should remain with the executive team. You present a vendor selection, and the board wants to interview the finalists. You recommend a control framework, and they debate specific tool configurations. You propose a budget allocation, and they redirect funds to projects they personally prefer.

In this case, the board does not trust executive judgment, or they have blurred the line between governance and execution. This often stems from a past incident that eroded confidence in management, or from directors who lack experience in distinguishing oversight from operations.

Recognition signals:

- The board asks for updates on routine operational matters (patch cycles, individual hires, ticket volumes).
- Directors cite practices at other companies to challenge your direction.
- You spend more time preparing board materials than managing your program.

How to respond: Raise it with your direct executive leader. Frame it as a governance boundary issue affecting execution: "I'm spending more time preparing board materials than running the program, and the level of operational detail they're requesting is slowing our response capability. Can we work with the CEO to reset expectations on what comes to the board versus what stays with management?"

If the issue doesn't get escalated, or it does and nothing changes, recognize the situation for what it is: the board doesn't trust management to operate independently. At that point, you're working around a structural problem, not solving it. That rarely ends well for the CISO.

The Messenger-Punishing Culture

In some organizations, boards react to bad news by blaming the person who delivered it. You report a control gap, and the board questions your competence. You escalate a vendor risk, and they ask why you approved the vendor in the first place. You present an incident, and they focus on who is accountable rather than how to recover.

When boards punish messengers, executives learn to withhold information, sugarcoat risks, and delay escalations. This creates a culture where the board receives only the news management thinks they can handle, not the news they need to govern effectively.

A board like this views accountability as blame rather than ownership. They have not distinguished between the person who reports a problem and the person who caused it.

Recognition signals:

- Executives soften bad news or delay reporting incidents to the board.

- Your peers advise you to "frame things more positively" before presenting.
- Board members focus on blame rather than response during incident discussions.
- You notice deteriorating trust after you've been transparent about challenges.

How to respond: This is one of the hardest cultures to change because it requires the board to recognize that its own behavior is counterproductive. You can attempt to address it with the CEO: "I want to ensure the board has complete visibility into our risk posture, but I'm concerned that transparency about challenges may be interpreted as management failure rather than good governance. How do we create space for candid risk reporting?" If the board continues to punish transparency, you face a choice: continue operating in an environment where honesty is career-limiting or find an organization that values governance over blame.

Political Crossfire: When Leadership Is Divided

Some of the most difficult board situations occur when the CEO and board chair are in conflict, when the board is divided into factions, or when individual directors are positioning for influence. In these environments, every update becomes political. Your technical recommendations get interpreted through the lens of who supports or opposes them. Presenting a budget request is no longer about cyber risk—it is about which faction controls resource allocation.

You may find yourself pressured to align with one side or the other. The CEO asks you to frame risk in ways that support their strategy. A board faction asks you to provide information that undermines the CEO's position. You are expected to navigate loyalties rather than present an objective risk assessment. The organization's leadership is fractured, and governance has broken down. In these environments, cybersecurity stops being the priority; power dynamics take over.

Recognition signals:

- Different executives give you conflicting guidance on how to frame the same issue.
- Board members ask you for information "off the record" or "just between us."
- Your updates trigger debates that have nothing to do with cybersecurity.
- You sense you are being evaluated based on which faction you support, not on your performance.

How to respond: Your only viable path is radical objectivity. Present risk as factually and neutrally as possible. Refuse to be drawn into political positioning. Document every recommendation you make. If pressured to take sides, escalate to the board chair or CEO and state clearly: "I'm being asked to provide information that feels more political than governance-focused. My role is to give the board an objective risk assessment. I want to make sure I'm fulfilling that responsibility appropriately." If the political environment does not resolve, recognize that your role has become untenable. No one succeeds in the long term when caught between competing power structures.

The Trust Gap That Cannot Be Repaired

Sometimes, a board loses confidence in a CISO, fairly or unfairly, and that confidence cannot be rebuilt. Maybe an incident happened on your watch, and the board believes it reflected poor judgment. Maybe you disagreed with a director in a way that damaged the relationship permanently. Maybe the board wanted to hire someone else, and you were the CEO's choice, creating ongoing tension.

When trust is gone, no amount of good performance, transparency, or alignment will restore it. The board will interpret everything you do through a lens of skepticism. Successes will be minimized. Challenges will be magnified. You will find yourself defending competence rather than demonstrating leadership.

In situations like this, the board has decided you are not the right person for the role. This may be fair, or it may reflect politics, personality conflict, or scapegoating. Either way, the outcome is the same.

Recognition signals:

- The board reduces your presentation time or moves your updates to the end of the agenda.
- Directors interrupt you more frequently and with a more hostile tone.
- Your recommendations are consistently questioned or overridden.
- You are excluded from strategic discussions you previously attended.
- The CEO stops defending you in board conversations.

How to respond: Have a direct conversation with the CEO: "I sense the board's confidence has shifted. Is there a path to rebuilding that trust, or should we discuss a transition?" If the CEO confirms that trust cannot be rebuilt, negotiate a graceful exit. Do not fight to stay in a role where the board does not support you. You will lose that battle, and it will damage your reputation in ways that affect future opportunities. If the CEO believes the board's loss of confidence is unfair but will not or cannot defend you effectively, recognize that you are in an unwinnable position. Leave on your terms rather than waiting to be pushed out.

How to Recognize When a Situation Is Career-Limiting

Not every difficult board dynamic is a reason to leave. Engaged boards challenge you. Skeptical boards test your thinking. Confrontational directors push you to be sharper. These are uncomfortable but often healthy dynamics that make you better at your job.

But some board cultures are fundamentally toxic. They punish transparency, micromanage execution, operate through political maneuvering, or have collectively decided you are not the right fit.

You should seriously consider leaving when any of the following things occur:

- The board consistently ignores your recommendations on material risks.
- You are being asked to misrepresent risk to support a predetermined narrative.
- The CEO will not or cannot protect you from board dysfunction.
- You spend more time managing board politics than managing cybersecurity.
- Your health, reputation, or personal values are being compromised.

These situations are not failures. They are mismatches. The board culture and your leadership style are incompatible. Recognizing that early and exiting strategically is a sign of professional maturity, not weakness.

A Final Note on Dysfunctional Boards

The scenarios described in this section represent a minority of boards. Most boards, even challenging ones, operate with professionalism, good faith, and a genuine desire to govern effectively. But dysfunctional boards exist, and they can be career-defining in negative ways if you do not recognize the patterns early.

Your responsibility is to attempt repair where possible: address misunderstandings, clarify boundaries, demonstrate competence, and build trust. But when repair is not possible, your responsibility shifts to protecting your career, your reputation, and your well-being. Know the difference between a board that is testing you and a board that has decided against you. One builds resilience. The other wastes time you cannot recover.

The best CISOs are not the ones who survive every board. They are the ones who recognize which boards are worth working for and which are not.

What to Carry Forward

- The boardroom is now central to your success as a CISO. Regulatory pressure, investor scrutiny, and a steady stream of companies in the news whose operations have been halted by cyberattacks have made cyber oversight a permanent board priority.
- Your role has expanded from operator to strategic advisor. Directors expect you to translate technical risk into business consequences.
- Directors evaluate your message through two lenses: fiduciary duty and strategic impact. Speak to both, or your message may not land.
- Body language and room dynamics tell you whether your framing is working. Learn to read the room in real time.
- Boards care about outcomes and confidence, not raw activity. Frame every issue in terms they use to govern risk, value, and reputation.

Chapter 3

Engineering Alignment: Before You Enter the Room

Your success with the board will rise or fall based on how well you collaborate before you enter the room. When executives show up with conflicting narratives, directors do not assume everyone has a valid perspective. They likely think the organization lacks unity, that the CEO is not integrating perspectives, and that the company may be exposed.

This chapter is about engineering alignment, so your board does not see multiple experts competing for airtime. You want them to see one leadership system. In Chapter 9, we'll go over presenting to the board in more detail.

The Risks of Misalignment

Boards interpret misalignment as a governance failure, not a communication glitch. When the CTO calls a transformation "strategic," the CFO calls it "burdensome," and the CISO calls it "risky," directors do not see nuance. They see a contradiction. They start asking: Who is right? Who is driving? Who is accountable?

Misalignment shows up in predictable ways:

- Separate slide decks prepared without collaboration
- Conflicting timelines for modernization and security readiness
- Budget requests that do not reflect shared priorities
- Different definitions of risk or maturity for the same initiative
- Escalations that skip one or more key leaders
- Conflicting characterizations of the same incident, such as "contained" versus "ongoing"

These are warning signals to those receiving the message. It is not only about technology; leadership and governance are also critical.

The Key Roles You Must Align With

Alignment is not a solo act. You cannot be successful in board communication in isolation as a CISO. You must understand how your peers see their responsibilities and how the board experiences them.

Figure 3.1 and the sections below describe the core roles most CISOs need to align with before every significant board interaction. Your organization may use different titles, but the functions are consistent.

The Chief Executive Officer

The CEO owns the strategy and the relationship with the board. Your job is to make it easy for them to demonstrate that technology and cyber risk are under disciplined control.

- Learn how the CEO talks about growth, transformation, and risk appetite.
- Frame your updates so they reinforce, not complicate, the CEO's strategic story.

- Avoid surprising the CEO with new risk narratives in the boardroom.

BOARDROOM SUCCESS IS ENGINEERED THROUGH EXECUTIVE ALIGNMENT

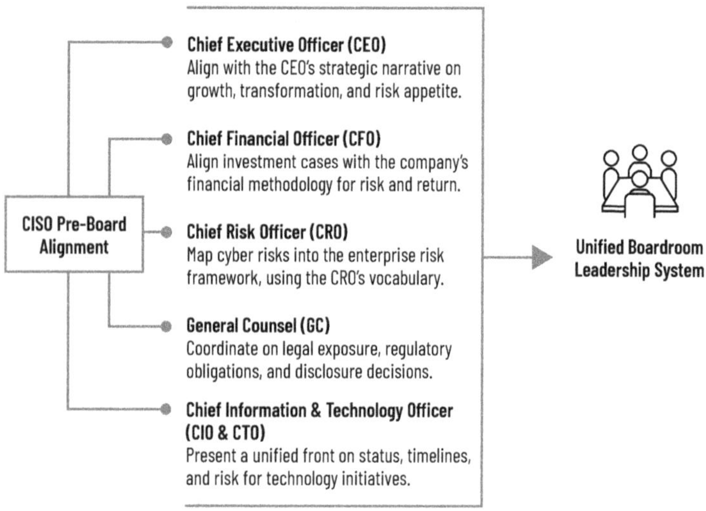

Figure 3.1. CISO executive alignment

The Chief Financial Officer

The CFO shapes how the board sees risk, return, and capital allocation. In many organizations, their perspective anchors the board's interpretation of every significant investment.

- Understand the company's financial methodology: how risk is modeled, how capital/operational expenditures are treated, and how returns are evaluated.
- Align your quantification and investment cases with the CFO's frameworks.

- Pre-align on ranges, assumptions, and trade-offs before you talk numbers with the board.

The Chief Risk Officer

Where a chief risk officer exists, they should be one of your closest allies. The CRO connects diverse risks into a single enterprise risk picture.

- Map your cyber risks into the CRO's enterprise risk categories and vocabulary.
- Ensure your risk reporting methodology, heat maps, ratings, and time horizons are consistent with theirs, or provide clear interpretation.
- Coordinate on which risks are escalated to the board, and how.

The General Counsel

The GC anchors legal exposure, regulatory obligations, and disclosure decisions. Misalignment with legal in front of the board is one of the fastest ways to lose credibility.

- Bring the GC into your thinking early on incidents, disclosures, AI governance, and material risk.
- Align on what can and should be said in open session versus closed session.
- When your recommendations carry legal support, everyone, especially the board, takes them more seriously.

The Chief Information Officer and Chief Technical Officer

The CIO and CTO are your primary partners in technology execution and innovation. In many organizations, you report to one of them. Regardless of structure, they are critical to your board narrative.

- CIOs generally own operational stability, availability, and infrastructure.
- CTOs generally own innovation, product technology, and delivery velocity.

Your independent lens is trust and assurance across both.

- Align on status, timelines, and dependencies for major initiatives.
- Ensure your risk framing reinforces, rather than contradicts, their updates.
- Agree on which of you leads which parts of the board conversation, and why.

These are not the only critical roles. Depending on the context of a given board update and your organizational structure, you may need tight alignment with business unit leaders, chief product officers, or even specific individual contributors for niche topics.

For material cyber incidents or public disclosures, you may also need to coordinate with communications and investor relations teams. These functions manage external messaging to media, customers, and investors. When an incident requires public disclosure, pre-align with them on timing, messaging, and how your technical briefing translates into external communications. Their expertise ensures consistency between what you tell the board and what stakeholders hear publicly. Know your landscape and plan accordingly.

The CISO's Position: Influence Without Territory

The CISO rarely owns every domain that touches digital risk. You do not run all of infrastructure, product engineering, or operations. Your influence comes from coordinating coherence, not from owning everything.

Ideally, boards see the CISO as the leader of organizational trust, who connects . . .

- Operational reality (CIO and operations)
- Innovation and product direction (CTO and product)
- Risk exposure and assurance (security, privacy, compliance)

. . . into one narrative of enterprise maturity.

That influence depends on three factors: clarity of responsibility, collaboration on narrative, and trust alignment.

Clarity of Responsibility

Map who owns execution, who owns innovation, and who owns assurance for key initiatives. Eliminate confusion about who does what and who speaks to which topics in the boardroom.

Collaboration on Narrative

Shape the board story together with the CIO and CTO, not in parallel. Review drafts, align language, and reconcile differences before assembling the board packet.

Trust Alignment

Interpret exposure, opportunity, and consequence in ways that connect all three roles:

- When you frame risk in ways that support innovation velocity, the CTO sees partnership.

- When you describe how assurance strengthens operational reliability, the CIO sees alignment.
- When you elevate uncertainty early and present options, the CEO sees maturity.

This is influence without territory and authority without full ownership.

The goal is to reach a state where the CIO and CTO don't see you as an auditor, but as a partner who helps them achieve their own goals safely. To get there, you must demonstrate that you understand their operational reality.

Power Dynamics and Political Reality

No leadership group operates without political tension. Budgets, visibility, and accountability create natural pressure. This can manifest in several ways:

- CIOs may feel threatened when CISOs appear more frequently before the board.
- CTOs may feel constrained when governance considerations influence delivery timelines.
- CISOs may feel sidelined when risk signals are deprioritized or softened.

These reactions are normal. What hurts organizations is silence. When tension is not acknowledged, leaders protect their own lanes rather than share responsibility.

Trust grows from partnership and transparency, not from budget battles fought in isolation.

Collaboration Patterns That Work

High-performing technology leadership teams do not rely on ad hoc coordination. They operate with predictable patterns that reduce friction and increase trust:

- Regular alignment sessions that include the CIO, CTO, CISO, and, as needed, the CEO, CFO, CRO, and GC.
- Shared dashboards that integrate availability, delivery, and key risk indicators into a single view.
- Joint preparation of board materials, especially for major initiatives or incidents.
- Consistent framing of transformation updates and risk signals, so directors hear a single story with multiple perspectives, not competing narratives.

These patterns create predictability, and predictability reduces friction. Directors can see the results of this collaboration in the clarity of the narrative and the coherence of the materials.

What to Carry Forward

- Technology leadership thrives when executives operate as a unified system rather than competing domains. While technical implementation matters, boards respond most strongly to strategic alignment that connects operations, innovation, and risk into a coherent narrative.
- Boards evaluate leadership maturity less by individual excellence and more by the seamless collaboration they witness

during presentations and discussions. The emergence of AI has only increased the need for this unified approach, as no single role can independently own its implementation, development, or governance.

- When breakdowns occur, they reveal more than technical gaps. They expose governance weaknesses that erode board confidence.

PART II

The Art of Translation

> *"You do not rise*
> *to the level of your goals.*
> *You fall to the level*
> *of your systems."*
>
> — James Clear

Chapter 4

Translating Cyber Risk

The audit chair just asked you a simple question: "Are we more secure than we were six months ago?"

You have the answer. Your team deployed multi-factor authentication across all customer accounts and implemented anomaly detection to flag suspicious login behavior. Last month alone, you blocked 127 account takeover attempts targeting high-value customers. Without those controls, attackers would have accessed payment information for roughly 240,000 customers.

But what you said was: "We implemented MFA with anomaly-based behavioral analytics and reduced successful account takeover attempts by 94 percent."

Silence.

The CFO looks confused. One director is checking email. The audit chair is still waiting for your answer to her question.

You just told them you prevented a breach that could have cost millions and destroyed customer trust. They heard acronyms and percentages.

Translation is not about simplifying risk. It is about making your message land for a new audience. The board rarely needs to know how ransomware propagates through your network. They need to understand what stops working if it hits, how much it costs to recover, what you need from them to reduce that risk, and how you will prevent it from happening again. That is translation.

This chapter is your field manual. It provides the frameworks, techniques, and examples you need to convert technical cyber risk into the business language directors use to govern. Master this, and you will transform board conversations from static updates to ones that drive organizational value.

Why Translation Failures Cost You

Most CISOs who struggle at the board level do not fail because they lack technical depth. They fail because they cannot explain why their work matters in terms the board understands. Here is what happens when interpretation breaks down:

- Budget cuts: Without a clear connection between your spending and business outcomes, finance sees your program as overhead. When budgets tighten, overhead gets cut.
- Misaligned priorities: If the board does not understand your risk framing, they will prioritize based on their own interpretation, which may not match reality.
- Crisis failures: When an incident hits, and you cannot quickly translate its impact, the board can lose confidence in your leadership.

In practice, translation is what separates CISOs who advise from those who report. One shapes strategy; the other doesn't.

The CISO's Translation Toolkit

These tools provide repeatable methods for translating technical risks into board language. Use them individually or combine them as needed.

The Three Questions Framework

You can improve your success in board conversations by addressing these three questions. If you can answer these clearly, you will secure alignment instead of prolonged debate:

1. **What could happen that would matter to the business?** Connect the risk to a specific outcome they care about, such as revenue loss, customer trust, regulatory penalty, or operational downtime.
2. **How likely is it, and what would it cost if it occurs?** Give them a clear sense of likelihood. Provide an impact range rather than a single number. Ranges are more credible than false precision.
3. **What are our options?** Present two or three paths with trade-offs. Make your recommendation clear. Tell them exactly what authorization or alignment you need to move forward.

This framework forces you to translate risk into governance-ready form. Directors want enough clarity and context to fulfill their oversight role, not a tour of your control stack.

The Business Language Dictionary

Replace security terminology with business outcomes. Use this reference (Table 4.1) as a starting point and adapt it to your organization.

Cyber Terminology	Translation
Confidentiality, integrity, availability	Data protection, accuracy of records, and service continuity
Data loss prevention	Controls that stop sensitive information from leaving the organization in an unauthorized way
Encryption	Protection that makes stolen data unreadable
Insider threat program	Monitoring and controls to detect malicious or negligent employee actions
Multi-factor authentication	Requires two proofs of identity and blocks most account compromises
Patch management	Closing known software weaknesses before they are exploited
Penetration testing	Simulated attack to find exploitable gaps before adversaries do
Security Operations Center	Team monitoring threats around the clock and responding to incidents
Threat intelligence	Early warning on adversary activity targeting our sector, which tells us where to apply resources
Zero trust architecture	Access is verified continuously, not granted permanently

The Quantification Approach

Financial numbers translate well with boards, but they will not trust quantification that looks made up. Your quantification must be transparent, evidence-based, and linked to an outcome.

How to quantify for results:

- Use impact ranges, not single-point estimates, for example, "three to six million dollars depending on recovery time."
- Ground estimates in reference events such as peer breaches, industry data breach reports, cyber insurance reports, and your own incident history.
- Show your assumptions and variables. If recovery time drives cost, say so.
- Separate direct costs, such as incident response, regulatory fines, and customer notification, from secondary effects, such as brand damage, customer churn, and lost deals.
- Connect the quantification to an outcome, for example, "therefore, we recommend investing X to reduce exposure by an estimated Y percent."
- Work with finance to refine your formulas and assumptions and be clear about capitalized versus operating costs. Align with the financial reports the board already sees.

What to avoid:

- Oddly precise figures, such as 4,872,340 dollars in expected loss. Directors know cyber risk is probabilistic, not deterministic.
- Quantification without context. Numbers alone do not drive direction; numbers tied to business outcomes do.
- Hiding uncertainty. If your estimate has a wide range, explain why. Transparency builds trust.

Translation in Action: Before and After Examples

The best way to understand translation is to see it work. Here are three common scenarios that show how technical framing fails and how business framing succeeds.

Example 1: Ransomware Risk

Before (technical framing)

"Our ransomware defenses include endpoint detection and response, immutable backups with 14-day retention, and network microsegmentation. We run monthly tabletop exercises and maintain a 96 percent patch compliance rate. Our mean time to detect is 4.2 hours."

After (business framing)

"If ransomware hits our core systems, we can restore critical operations within 6 hours and full operations within 24 hours—that limits revenue impact per incident. We invested 2.1 million dollars across backups, endpoint detection, and incident readiness last year to achieve this level of resilience. Without it, a similar attack could cost us 8–15 million dollars and take three to five weeks to recover, based on claims data and public disclosures from peers in our sector."

Why this works

The second version tells the board what they care about: recovery time, revenue impact, and how your investment reduced exposure and improved resilience. Details on microsegmentation are not required here. They need to know you can restore the business quickly and that their investment improves assurance.

Example 2: Vulnerability Management

Before (technical framing)
"We scan 8,400 endpoints weekly and track 1,200 open vulnerabilities. Our CVSS score distribution shows 15% critical, 35% high, and 50% medium. Mean time to remediate critical CVEs is 18 days."

After (business framing)
"We prioritize vulnerabilities based on which systems they threaten. Right now, there are 22 high-severity weaknesses in systems that support our customer-facing payment platform. We are closing those within 10 days. Another 180 affect internal systems with lower business impact, and those are patched within 30 days. This aligns with a risk-based approach that focuses our resources on protecting revenue systems first."

Why this works

The second version maps vulnerabilities to business impact, for example, payment platforms and revenue, and shows how you prioritize. Directors understand resource trade-offs, even if the Common Vulnerability Scoring System and the Common Vulnerabilities and Exposures system are foreign.

Example 3: Third-Party Risk

Before (technical framing)

"We conducted security assessments on 47 vendors this quarter using our third-party risk management framework. Twelve vendors scored below 70 on our maturity scale. We are requiring

SOC 2 reports from all Tier 1 vendors and conducting annual penetration tests on critical integrations."

After (business framing)

"Three of our logistics vendors handle data for 60 percent of our shipments, and two of them have significant security gaps. If either of those vendors suffers a breach, we could lose visibility into shipments across the Midwest for 24–48 hours, delaying deliveries and triggering customer service escalations. We are working with them to close those gaps within 90 days. If they cannot meet that timeline, I recommend we work with the business owners to evaluate backup vendors."

Why this works

The second version identifies the business dependency (shipments and regional coverage), quantifies the exposure (24–48 hours of disruption), and frames a clear direction (close gaps or identify alternatives). This is risk the board can govern.

What to Carry Forward

- Translation is the skill that can elevate you from the cyber leader to a board-trusted business leader. It is not about simplifying your message; it is about making it actionable.
- When you translate technical risk into business language, you help the board govern. When you help them govern, you earn their trust. When you earn their trust, you gain influence

over the approvals that shape your program and your organization.

- Use the frameworks in this chapter every time you prepare a board presentation, respond to a director's question, or frame a cyber risk for executive leadership. Translation is a muscle. The more you use it, the stronger it gets.
- Other chapters will reference the concepts here, including vocabulary, quantification, and the associated frameworks. This chapter is your source material. Come back to it when you need to sharpen your approach or connect cyber protection to business performance.

Chapter 5

Governance: Frameworks That Speak to Boards

The audit chair asks a question you should have seen coming: "We just approved $250,000 for NIST and ISO work. Explain to me what we're buying."

You've been in a leadership role for six years and know these frameworks cold. But standing in front of the board, you realize you have never actually explained what frameworks like these achieve in language that matters to directors.

You start talking. "NIST CSF organizes cybersecurity into six functions: Govern, Identify, Protect, Detect, Respond, and Recover. It has implementation tiers that measure maturity. ISO 27001 is an international standard for information security management systems that requires documentation, audit, and certification. Together they provide..."

The CFO interrupts. "I still don't know what we're buying. Are we buying better security? Are we buying proof that we have good security? Are we checking a compliance box?"

The audit chair tries to help. "Let me ask it differently. If we don't do this, what happens? Do we have more risk? Do we fail an audit? Do we lose customers?"

You know the answer. Regulators will ask what framework we follow. Auditors will flag governance gaps. Customers will require certification. Insurance carriers will question our maturity. But you've never put all of that together into a single story that shows the board why frameworks are the language everyone uses to judge how you're managing cyber risk.

As you can see from this interaction, boards need proof of systematic oversight; words and slides are not enough. Frameworks provide that proof in a language that regulators, auditors, and investors understand. Your job as CISO is to translate the value of frameworks like the National Institute of Standards and Technology Cybersecurity Framework (NIST CSF) and International Organization for Standardization/International Electrotechnical Commission 27001 (ISO/IEC 27001) into board confidence.

What Governance Means in Cybersecurity

Governance answers three questions:

- Who decides?
- Who acts?
- Who assures?

Put simply, governance is about accountability and oversight, not technical controls.

- The board governs by setting direction, risk appetite, and expectations.
- Executives direct by allocating resources and setting priorities.
- Operations are executed by implementing controls and managing day-to-day activities.

Frameworks make this structure visible and auditable. They create clear ownership and demonstrate that someone is accountable for every cyber risk. They show regulators and auditors that cybersecurity is managed systematically, not reactively.

In Chapter 2, we explored how boards think about oversight and fiduciary duty. In Chapter 4, we focused on how to translate technical risk into business language. Governance frameworks bridge those concepts. They give you a common vocabulary to discuss accountability, maturity, exposure, resilience, and assurance with directors who may not understand next-generation firewalls but absolutely understand organizational structure and responsibility.

When a regulator asks, "Who is accountable for cyber risk?" or an auditor asks, "How do you ensure controls are working?", frameworks provide the answer. They show that cybersecurity is not just an IT function. It is a managed business capability with clear ownership, from the board down to operations.

Governance without frameworks is abstract. Frameworks without governance are just documentation. Together, they create the foundation for board confidence.

Why Frameworks Matter to Boards: The Business Case

Directors do not care about frameworks because they are technically elegant. They care because frameworks reduce risk and demonstrate due diligence. In practice, this matters because every external party scrutinizing your organization—regulators, auditors, investors, insurers, and courts—evaluates your cyber posture through the lens of recognized frameworks.

Regulators

The SEC, Federal Trade Commission (FTC), banking regulators, and state authorities increasingly reference frameworks in guidance and enforcement actions. After major breaches, they ask,

"What framework did you use? How did you measure maturity? Who was accountable?" Organizations without a framework-based governance structure can face more challenging questions and greater scrutiny.

Auditors

External and internal auditors use frameworks as benchmarks. ISO/IEC 27001 provides certification criteria. NIST CSF provides maturity tiers. Control Objectives for Information and Related Technologies (COBIT) provides a governance structure. When auditors can map your program to a recognized framework, audits go faster, and findings are clearer.

Investors and acquirers

Private equity firms, venture capitalists, and strategic buyers now treat cybersecurity as standard due diligence. One of the first questions is, "What frameworks do you follow?" Framework adoption signals maturity. Certifications such as ISO 27001 or SOC 2 can accelerate deals and reduce friction.

Cyber insurers

Underwriters use frameworks to assess risk. Organizations with mature NIST CSF implementations or ISO 27001 certification are often viewed more favorably. Frameworks show you manage risk systematically, which reduces the insurer's exposure.

Courts and enforcement

In litigation or regulatory action, boards are judged on whether they exercised reasonable care in overseeing cyber risk. Aligning with frameworks provides evidence of that care. They show the board established oversight structures, allocated resources, and monitored performance.

Four Major Frameworks Explained in Board Language

Most CISOs know these frameworks. Most boards do not. Your job is to translate what each framework does and why it matters to governance.

This section is the canonical reference for framework education. Later chapters will reference it rather than re-explain frameworks.

Note: Many other frameworks exist, including sector-specific or mandated ones. Here, I focus on COBIT, NIST CSF, ISO 27001, and CIS Controls because, together, they form a complementary system that boards can understand.

COBIT 2019: The Governance Foundation

COBIT (Control Objectives for Information and Related Technologies) is an enterprise framework for IT governance and management, developed by the Information Systems Audit and Control Association (ISACA). It is not specific to cybersecurity. It covers the entire IT domain and provides the governance structure within which cybersecurity programs operate.

Why boards care:

COBIT maps governance activities to three core functions:

- Evaluate: understand risk and performance.
- Direct: set objectives and allocate resources.
- Monitor: verify results and assurance.

This is how boards already think about their oversight role.

When to use:

- When the board wants a clear governance structure
- When regulators or auditors ask, "Who is accountable for cyber risk?"
- When you need to demonstrate that cybersecurity decisions have clear ownership and oversight

NIST Cybersecurity Framework 2.0: The Management Lens

The NIST Cybersecurity Framework (CSF) is a risk management framework developed by the National Institute of Standards and Technology. It organizes cybersecurity activities into six core functions: Govern, Identify, Protect, Detect, Respond, and Recover.

Why boards care:

NIST CSF is one of the most widely adopted frameworks in the United States, and regulators frequently reference it. It enables comparison across organizations and industries.

The six functions create a complete cyber risk management lifecycle:

- Govern: establish and monitor cybersecurity strategy and risk management.
- Identify: understand assets, risks, and business context.
- Protect: implement safeguards to limit impact.
- Detect: discover cybersecurity events quickly.
- Respond: contain and mitigate incidents.
- Recover: restore capabilities and services.

NIST also defines four maturity tiers:

Tier 1: Partial
Cybersecurity is reactive and ad hoc, with limited awareness of risk across the organization.

Tier 2: Risk Informed
Risk management practices exist and are approved by leadership, but implementation is inconsistent across the organization.

Tier 3: Repeatable
Formal policies are in place, regularly updated, and consistently implemented organization-wide.

Tier 4: Adaptive
The organization continuously learns from threats and incidents, adapts defenses proactively, and integrates cyber risk into enterprise strategy.

When to use:

- U.S.-based companies or those subject to U.S. regulatory expectations
- Organizations seeking a risk-based, business-aligned approach
- Companies that want a framework they can use to track exposure, resilience, and assurance over time

ISO/IEC 27001: The Assurance Standard

International Organization for Standardization/International Electrotechnical Commission standard 27001 (ISO/IEC 27001, or ISO 27001) is the international standard for information security management systems (ISMSs). It defines requirements for establishing, implementing, maintaining, and continually improving an ISMS.

Why boards care:

ISO 27001 is globally recognized and third-party certified. Certification provides independent proof that your controls work. Many customers and partners require ISO 27001 certification by contract.

A core concept is the continuous improvement cycle:

- Plan (Clauses 4–6): Establish the ISMS, define scope and policies, assess risks
- Do (Clauses 7–8): Implement controls and processes
- Check (Clause 9): Monitor, measure, and analyze through audits and management reviews
- Act (Clause 10): Take corrective actions and drive continual improvement

ISO 27001 requires documented processes, regular audits, management reviews, and corrective actions. Certification involves an independent auditor verifying compliance.

When to use:

- Global operations or international customers
- Customer or partner requirements for certification
- Situations where third-party validation provides a competitive advantage

CIS Critical Security Controls: The Implementation Layer

The CIS Controls are a prioritized set of 18 safeguards developed by the Center for Internet Security. They are tactical and specific, covering everything from asset inventory to incident response. CIS organizes controls into three Implementation Groups (IG1, IG2, IG3) based on size and maturity.

Why boards care:

CIS Controls are practical and prioritized. They show efficient resource allocation. Instead of trying to do everything at once, you focus on controls that deliver the most risk reduction first. For boards focused on budget and ROI, CIS demonstrates disciplined investment.

Implementation Groups:

- IG1: Essential controls for smaller or less mature organizations
- IG2: Additional controls for organizations with moderate IT resources
- IG3: Advanced controls for organizations facing sophisticated threats

When to use:

- Operational implementation and control design
- Resource prioritization and quick wins
- Showing the board that every dollar of security spend is targeted at high-impact areas

How Frameworks Work Together: The Hierarchy

These frameworks are not competing. They are complementary. Each answers a different governance question. (see Figure 5.1.)

You can think of them as a stack:

- COBIT (governance) defines who decides, who acts, and who assures.
- NIST CSF (management) defines what you manage and how you measure maturity.
- ISO 27001 (assurance) validates that your management system works through independent certification.
- CIS Controls (implementation) define which specific controls to implement and in what order.

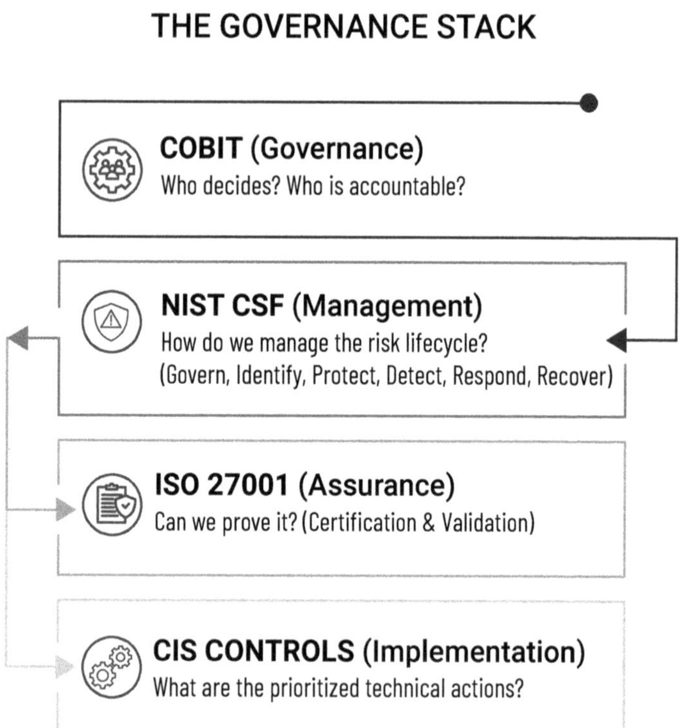

Figure 5.1. The governance stack

Each framework answers a different governance question. Together, they demonstrate systematic cybersecurity management at every level, from board oversight to daily operations.

Presenting Frameworks to Boards: Translation Techniques

In Chapter 4, we covered how to translate cyber risk into business language. The same principles apply here.

Lead With Value, Not Structure

Bad approach:

"NIST CSF has six functions and 106 subcategories across four tiers . . ."

Better approach:

"NIST CSF helps us manage cyber risk the way we manage financial risk: with clear processes, measurable maturity, and industry benchmarks that regulators recognize."

Boards need the outcome, not the internal wiring.

Use Board Language, Not Framework Jargon

Framework jargon:

"We are at NIST Tier 2, with partial implementation of the Govern function."

Board language:

"We have structured, repeatable processes for managing cyber risk in most areas, and we are now formalizing governance so that oversight is consistent across all business units. That will make M&A reviews faster and align with what our cyber insurer expects to see."

Connect Frameworks to Business Outcomes

Every framework story should answer the question, "What business outcome does this enable?"

- Outcome framing: "NIST helps us manage cyber risk with the same rigor we apply to financial risk."
- Regulatory framing: "ISO 27001 certification satisfies customer security requirements and strengthens our position with regulators."
- Efficiency framing: "CIS Controls prioritize investments, so we reduce the most risk with the least spend."
- Assurance framing: "COBIT shows clear accountability to regulators when they ask who is responsible for cyber risk."

What Not to Do

- Do not walk through the full structure of NIST, COBIT, ISO, or CIS.
- Do not use acronyms without explanation.
- Do not show maturity scores without context ("Tier 2" alone means nothing).
- Do not assume directors are familiar with frameworks. Many are not.

What to Do

- Lead with business value and start with outcomes, not structure.
- Use analogies: "NIST is like generally accepted accounting principles for cybersecurity, a common language for managing risk."
- Show how frameworks reduce specific risks or costs.
- Connect frameworks directly to board priorities: compliance, risk reduction, reputation, and efficiency.

Directors do not need to become framework experts. They need to understand why frameworks matter and how you are using them to manage exposure, resilience, and assurance systematically.

Common Board Questions About Frameworks (and How to Answer Them)

Boards ask predictable questions. Prepare for them.

Q1: "Which framework should we use?"
Answer: "It depends on three factors: regulatory requirements, customer expectations, and our maturity level. Most organizations use a combination. For us, I recommend [frameworks] because [business rationale: regulatory alignment, customer needs, practical implementation]. As we mature, we can add [additional frameworks] to close specific gaps."

Q2: "How much will this cost?"
Answer: "Framework adoption has three cost components: initial assessment, implementation, and ongoing maintenance. For this program, we expect an initial investment of approximately [X]

over [Y] months. The return comes from lower regulatory risk, potential reductions in cyber insurance premiums, and faster customer or M&A due diligence. We will report progress and ROI using clear metrics."

Q3: "Are we compliant with this framework?"
Answer: "Compliance is not binary; it is a maturity journey. Today we are at [current state], with roughly [percentage] of key controls implemented. Our target is [future state] by [date], aligned to [business goal]. We will report progress quarterly using maturity and performance metrics tied to business outcomes."

Q4: "Do our competitors use this framework?"
Answer: "Most organizations in our sector use some combination of NIST, ISO, COBIT, and CIS. These have become expectations in regulatory reviews, customer assessments, and requests for proposals. Not aligning to them would put us at a disadvantage in areas such as regulatory standing and customer trust."

Q5: "How do we know it is working?"
Answer: "We measure effectiveness through three lenses: independent audits (external validation), control testing results (internal assurance), and incident response performance (real-world outcomes). We will report those results regularly so you can see how framework adoption improves over time."

Q6: "Can we get certified?"
Answer: "ISO 27001 offers formal certification, which many customers require. NIST and COBIT do not provide certification in the same way, but we can benchmark our maturity against them. ISO

27001 certification typically takes 8 months and costs approximately $175k. The business value is better customer access, stronger regulatory posture, and a clearer story for investors and partners."

Framework Maturity and Roadmap Discussions

Boards need to see progress, not just labels. Avoid "maturity theater."

Inflating maturity scores to look good will erode trust when incidents occur. Honest assessment builds credibility.

Maturity Communication Framework

Every maturity discussion should include five elements:

- **Current state:** Where we are today, with an honest assessment
- **Target state:** Where we need to be, aligned to risk appetite and business goals
- **Gap analysis:** What is missing, prioritized by risk
- **Roadmap:** How we get there, including timeline, resources, and milestones
- **Business value:** Why it matters, framed in outcomes rather than activities

Here's an example of a board-ready maturity update:

"We are currently at NIST Tier 2, Risk Informed. We have structured processes for managing cyber risk, but they are not yet fully repeatable across all business units. Our target is Tier 3, Repeatable, by [date], which will enable faster M&A reviews, support our insurance program, and demonstrate systematic oversight to regulators. The primary gaps are governance oversight, vendor risk management, and supply chain security. We are addressing them through three initiatives over the next 18 months. We will report progress quarterly using metrics tied to reduced exposure, improved resilience, and clearer assurance."

Governance Structures and Accountability

Frameworks provide the language. Governance structures provide accountability.

The Four Layers of Governance

Effective cyber governance operates at four levels:

1. Board oversight
- Sets risk appetite and strategic direction
- Approves significant investments and policy changes
- Monitors performance through committees
- Holds executives accountable for results

2. Executive direction
- Translates board direction into concrete priorities and resource allocation
- Approves policies, standards, and major initiatives
- Escalates material risks to the board
- Ensures cross-functional alignment across IT, legal, finance, operations, and others

3. Management execution
- Implements policies and standards
- Manages day-to-day security operations
- Reports performance and risk to executives
- Identifies and escalates emerging risks

4. Operational implementation
• Executes specific controls and procedures
• Monitors systems and responds to incidents
• Documents and reports control effectiveness
• Provides feedback for continuous improvement

Transparent layers prevent gaps and overlaps. Everyone knows who decides, who acts, and who assures. When an incident occurs, accountability is visible. See Figure 5.2 for an overview.

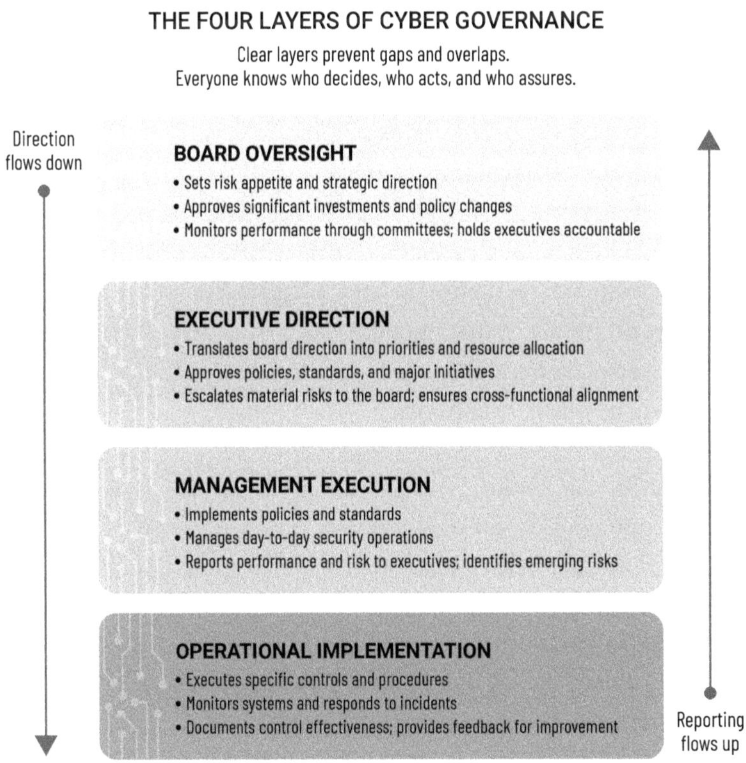

Figure 5.2. The four layers of cyber governance

You rarely inherit a perfect structure. Acquisitions, leadership changes, and budget politics all complicate governance. Your job is not to design a textbook-perfect chart. It is to move toward accountability and to help the board understand how better governance improves business outcomes.

Reporting Lines and Escalation Paths

Information must flow logically between layers.

- Routine briefings: Monthly or quarterly executive updates that align operations with board priorities
- Defined escalation triggers: Pre-agreed criteria that specify when to alert the board, for example:
    - Material financial impact above a set threshold
    - Regulatory exposure that may trigger disclosure
    - Significant reputational risk, such as customer data exposure
    - Operational disruption beyond an agreed duration
- Crisis protocols: A documented chain of contact that includes who leads communication, who authorizes disclosure, and how quickly updates are expected

Escalation is not failure. It is proof that governance works. Directors gain confidence when serious issues surface through disciplined channels, early, and with a plan attached. If you present everything as perfect all the time, your requests will be scrutinized more heavily, and real incidents will be more damaging to your credibility.

Integration with Enterprise Risk Management

Cyber risk is enterprise risk. It should be managed alongside financial, operational, and strategic risks in the same system.

Key integration elements:

- **Risk appetite:** The board sets acceptable exposure levels for cyber risk alongside other risks.
- **Enterprise risk register:** Cyber risks are mapped to business functions and included in the central register.
- **Metrics and key risk indicators (KRIs):** Cyber metrics are reported alongside other enterprise metrics, using the same cadence and format.
- **Feedback loops:** Incidents, control testing, and external assessments all feed back into enterprise risk decisions.

When cyber risk is integrated with enterprise risk management, it stops being an "IT issue" and becomes part of how the organization stabilizes operations, enables performance, and assures stakeholders.

What to Carry Forward

- Frameworks are not technical checklists. They are governance tools that demonstrate systematic oversight.
- When boards see frameworks as part of a disciplined system for managing exposure, resilience, and assurance, they stop viewing cybersecurity as a black box. They see a managed capability that sits alongside financial and operational governance.
- Your ability to translate framework value into board confidence determines your influence. Directors who understand why frameworks matter become strong advocates for resources, prioritization, and strategic alignment.

Chapter 6

Regulatory Compliance: Speaking the Language of Legal Risk

The quarterly board meeting was running smoothly. The CFO had walked through earnings. The chief operating officer covered operational updates. Your cybersecurity report was next on the agenda, tucked between strategy and risk committee updates. You had prepared your standard compliance summary: GDPR controls validated, no material findings from the last round of audits. Straightforward.

Then the board chair leaned forward. "Before we move on, I have a question." The room went quiet. "Will we be blindsided by a regulator citing us for something we didn't know about or didn't fix in time?"

You felt every director's eyes shift to you. Direct question. Complex answer.

The honest answer requires nuance. The company operates in 14 states and six countries. Each jurisdiction has different data privacy laws, breach notification timelines, and enforcement priorities. Three state privacy laws changed in the last six months. The EU keeps issuing new guidance on cross-border data transfers. China's data localization requirements are evolving. Your compliance team tracks it all, but regulatory change moves faster than most governance cycles, and "compliant" is not a static state. It is a moving target that requires constant monitoring, interpretation, and gap remediation.

You have two choices. You can give the reassuring answer: "We have strong monitoring processes in place, and I'm confident we'll catch regulatory changes in time." That answer is what they want to hear, but it is incomplete. Or you can give the realistic answer: "We monitor regulatory changes actively and have remediation processes, but I cannot guarantee we will never be caught off-guard. Regulations shift constantly, enforcement priorities are unpredictable, and interpretation varies by jurisdiction. What I can tell you is how we monitor, how we prioritize gaps, and how quickly we respond when we find issues." That answer is honest, but it might sound like hedging.

The board chair is still looking at you. The general counsel is watching. You have about ten seconds to decide how to frame this.

Every CISO has faced some version of that moment. The question is not really about statutes or acronyms. It is about whether the board can demonstrate control when scrutiny arrives. For directors, compliance has become a proxy for regulatory competence, and the CISO now owns a significant part of that narrative.

Transparency under pressure builds trust. Boards can help close gaps when they are informed early.

Why Regulatory Compliance Matters to the Board

Five years ago, privacy and cybersecurity regulations lived in legal or audit committees. Today, they headline board agendas. The catalyst was not just enforcement; it was liability.

Personal Accountability Has Arrived

When the SEC approved its 2023 cybersecurity disclosure rules, it formally placed boards inside the accountability loop. Public companies must now disclose material cyber incidents within four business days and report annually on their cyber risk governance structures. The message to boards was unambiguous: cyber oversight is no longer optional or something you can delegate. It is a fiduciary duty.

Then came the cascade of privacy laws: GDPR in Europe, the California Consumer Privacy Act (CCPA) and California Privacy Rights Act (CPRA) in California, and similar statutes rippling through U.S. states and global markets. Each carries cross-border implications and enforcement mechanisms. Directors quickly absorbed the message: regulatory exposure is not a function of IT hygiene. It is a test of governance maturity.

Compliance as Reputation Insurance

For boards, the real risk is more than the financial fine; it is the headline. In recent years, organizations across financial services, healthcare, retail, and technology have faced enforcement actions, executive departures, and hundreds of millions of dollars in settlements tied to compliance failures. In most cases, the underlying vulnerabilities were known, and the regulatory obligations were clear. What was missing was the governance discipline to close gaps before regulators arrived. The pattern is consistent: a breach occurs, investigators determine that a known weakness went unaddressed, regulators impose penalties, and boards face questions about whether they exercised reasonable oversight. The financial penalties are significant, but the lasting damage is reputational. Customers, investors, and partners interpret a compliance failure as a signal that leadership was not paying attention. For directors, that perception is harder to recover from than the fine itself.

The CISO's Expanded Role

The board's question has shifted from "Are we compliant?" to "Can we prove it, and can we adapt when the rules change?"

That shift repositioned the CISO from technical operator to governance translator. The general counsel interprets the law; the CISO demonstrates control. Together, they give the board confidence that regulatory discipline is embedded in how the company operates, reports, and responds.

Overview Of Major Regulations: What the Board Needs to Hear

When a director asks, "How are we aligned with GDPR, CCPA, and the SEC rules?" they are not asking for a legal memo. They are signaling a duty: the board must demonstrate reasonable oversight across overlapping mandates.

Your role in that moment is to decipher each regulatory regime into its implications for risk posture, accountability, and communication with investors and regulators.

Below are the regulations that most often show up in the boardroom.

Note: There are many other regulations where the CISO is an owner or a supporting player. The point of this chapter is not to teach you all of them. It is to show you how the board views them and how to communicate in a way that directors will value.

GDPR (General Data Protection Regulation): The Global Accountability Benchmark

For most directors, GDPR is not just "that EU privacy law." It is the standard against which data protection regulation is measured. Effective since 2018, GDPR applies to any organization that processes personal data of EU residents, regardless of where the company is based.

What it means for boards: Any organization that handles EU personal data must meet strict expectations for how that data is collected, used, and protected. Penalties can reach 20 million euros or four percent of global revenue, whichever is higher. While the regulation does not impose personal fines on executives or directors, it does expect boards to oversee data protection with the same rigor they apply to financial and operational risk.

Board framing: "GDPR established the expectation that privacy is a direct extension of corporate governance, not an IT or legal function."

Key board questions the CISO should address:

- Accountability structure: Who owns data protection internally, and can we demonstrate that ownership to regulators?
- Cross-border implications: Do our global operations elevate exposure through data transfers or third-party vendors?
- Breach disclosure discipline: Can our incident response meet the 72-hour breach notification requirement?

The board does not need the implementation details. It needs assurance that these questions have clear, defensible answers.

CCPA/CPRA (California Consumer Privacy Act/California Privacy Rights Act)

California was the first state to bring GDPR-style rights and obligations into the U.S. market. CCPA took effect in 2020, and CPRA strengthened it in 2023. The law applies to any business, regardless of location, that does business with California residents and meets certain thresholds: $25 million in annual revenue, handling data from 100,000 or more California residents, or deriving 50% of revenue from selling personal information. The regulatory structure differs from Europe, but the impact on the board is similar: privacy has become a visible signal of consumer trust, brand risk, and investor scrutiny.

What it means for boards: These laws give consumers enforceable rights to access, delete, and opt out of the sale of their personal information. Violations can trigger regulatory action, class-action lawsuits, and reputational harm that shows up in earnings calls and analyst reports.

Board framing: "California regulators turned privacy violations into headlines. The brand damage, not just the fine, is the real loss."

Key board questions the CISO should address:

- How does the company manage consumer opt-out rights and data requests without disrupting business operations?
- How are privacy obligations incorporated into customer experience and marketing, where most exposure originates?
- Are we monitoring regulatory movement in other states that mirror California's structure?

Here, the communication emphasis shifts from legal definitions to brand defense through compliance.

U.S. State Privacy Laws: The Patchwork Challenge

Many U.S. states (and growing) have comprehensive privacy laws. They follow a familiar pattern of consumer rights and data governance duties, but each includes differences in scope and enforcement. California set the trajectory, and states such as Virginia, Colorado, Connecticut, Utah, and others have created a fragmented privacy landscape that continues to expand.

What it means for boards: The risk is not any single law; it is inconsistency across multiple jurisdictions. Organizations operating in multiple states must manage overlapping and sometimes conflicting obligations without a federal standard to unify them.

Board framing: "Our compliance challenge is not complexity in any one state; it is maintaining consistency across all of them."

Key board questions the CISO should address:

- Do we have a system to detect and map new state obligations as they pass?
- How quickly can we synchronize compliance updates across product lines and geographies?
- Can we provide regular assurance reports summarizing "change absorbed vs. change pending"?

SEC Cybersecurity Disclosure Rules: From Governance to Public Accountability

The SEC's cybersecurity disclosure rules became effective in December 2023 for most public companies, with smaller reporting companies following in June 2024. The rules apply to public companies subject to the Exchange Act, including Foreign Private Issuers. The rules require two key items: material cyber incidents must be disclosed on Form 8-K within four business days of determining that the incident is material (not four days from discovery, but from the materiality determination), and annual reports must describe the board's oversight of cybersecurity risk.

Board impact: This regulation transformed cybersecurity oversight from an internal governance matter into an investor relations function. Board-level risk centers on investor confidence, analyst scrutiny, and regulatory enforcement tied to disclosure failures. The quality of cyber governance is now publicly disclosed and scrutinized.

Board framing: "The SEC turned cybersecurity oversight into a disclosure obligation. Our governance discipline is now a matter of public record."

Key board questions the CISO should address:

- Can we detect and assess materiality fast enough to meet the four-day disclosure requirement?
- Can we demonstrate that cyber risk is embedded in the board's governance rhythm rather than handled as an ad hoc discussion?
- If we filed an 8-K tomorrow, would it demonstrate disciplined governance or raise more questions than it answers?

HIPAA (Health Insurance Portability and Accountability Act): Healthcare's Baseline

For healthcare organizations, HIPAA is the foundational privacy and security regulation. Enforced by the U.S. Department of Health and Human Services, HIPAA mandates safeguards for protected health information (PHI) and imposes penalties for violations.

What it means for boards: HIPAA violations can result in tiered fines, with an annual maximum exceeding $2 million dollars per violation category. The larger exposure is reputational. Breaches often become public, create patient distrust, and trigger litigation.

Board framing: "HIPAA compliance is not optional in healthcare. Breaches signal both technical failure and governance gaps."

Key board questions the CISO should address:

- Are our safeguards for protected health information operating effectively and tested regularly?

- Can we detect, contain, and report a PHI breach within the required regulatory timeframes?
- Do we have evidence that our HIPAA obligations are met across all systems, partners, and workflows that handle patient data?

SOX (Sarbanes-Oxley Act): Financial Integrity Meets Cybersecurity

While SOX is primarily a financial reporting regulation, Section 404 requires public companies to maintain adequate internal controls over financial reporting.

What it means for boards: Cyber incidents that compromise financial data or reporting systems can trigger SOX violations, auditor concerns, and investor scrutiny. Boards must ensure that cybersecurity controls are tested and auditable as part of SOX compliance.

Board framing: "SOX requires us to prove that our financial controls are reliable, and cybersecurity is now part of that proof."

Key board questions the CISO should address:

- Can we demonstrate that our financial reporting systems are protected, monitored, and resilient against cyber disruption?
- Do we have evidence that our SOX-relevant cybersecurity controls are operating effectively?
- If a cyber incident affects financial data, how quickly would we detect it, contain it, and assess materiality for disclosure?

Compliance Versus Frameworks: Clarifying the Distinction

One source of confusion in board discussions is the line between regulatory compliance and governance frameworks.

The distinction is simple:

- Regulations are mandatory. They are laws, standards, or contractual obligations with legal or financial consequences for non-compliance. GDPR, CCPA, SEC rules, HIPAA, and SOX fall into this category.
- Frameworks are voluntary. They are structured approaches to governance and risk management that help organizations meet regulatory requirements and industry best practices. NIST Cybersecurity Framework, ISO 27001, COBIT, and CIS Controls fall into this category.

In practice, most organizations use frameworks (covered in detail in Chapter 5) to build governance structures that satisfy multiple regulatory requirements at once. Your job is to show the board how the governance framework supports compliance, without confusing the two.

Board framing: "We use the NIST Cybersecurity Framework to organize our security program. That program ensures we meet GDPR, CCPA, SEC, and industry-specific regulatory requirements. The framework is how we govern; the regulations are what we must satisfy."

This distinction helps directors understand that frameworks are tools, not obligations, and that they are used strategically to efficiently meet regulatory requirements.

Note: This comparison may feel obvious to you, but many executives and directors do get confused here. Having a simple explanation ready saves time and reduces friction.

Presenting Regulatory Compliance Status to the Board

Spending 10 minutes explaining how robust your regulatory compliance program is will not go over well. What matters most is a clear message that shows results. Complexity in your wording often signals uncertainty.

Boards do not need reassurance. They need orientation. They want to know three things:

- Where we stand: Our current posture against key obligations.
- What is changing: New or emerging regulations that affect our exposure or obligations.
- What is at stake: The consequences if we lag behind, in terms of exposure, resilience, and assurance.

If you organize every slide or sentence around that triad, you will gain immediate clarity.

Structure That Directors Remember

Effective board reporting follows the rhythm directors already know from financial oversight. Use headings that sound like leadership, not legal text:

- Context: What regulation or disclosure duty matters this quarter?
- Status: Confidence level with a one-line rationale.
- Trend: Are we improving or slipping?
- Impact: What the movement means for business or reputation.
- Next step/ask: What approvals or investments does leadership need?

Boards appreciate disciplined storytelling: a stable template, consistent metrics, and transparent movement over time.

Metrics That Work at the Board Level

Three categories of metrics resonate most with directors:

- Regulatory coverage: What percentage of applicable regulations have identified owners, controls, and evidence repositories?
- Change velocity: How quickly can we absorb new regulatory requirements? For example, the average time from regulation passage to control implementation.
- Assurance readiness: How many of our key compliance assertions are validated by external audit or independent review?

You can describe these as your compliance lens on exposure, resilience, and assurance: coverage shapes exposure, change velocity reflects resilience, and assurance readiness reflects assurance.

Keep these metrics persistent across quarters. Boards gain trust from visual stability. What changes is the storyline, not the indicators.

Framing Non-Compliance with Transparency

One of the hardest, yet most credibility-building, moments for a CISO is admitting non-compliance. Boards do not expect perfection. They expect visibility and control.

Replace anxiety with accountability.

Instead of "We are still working on full CCPA alignment," say, "We are about 75 percent aligned with CCPA. The remaining gaps are vendor contract clauses and employee data handling procedures. Completion is targeted for Q2. We see no customer-facing exposure from the remaining work."

That statement projects calm precision, not defensiveness. The board hears capability, not crisis.

Translation Techniques (Applying Chapter 4 principles)

In Chapter 4, we covered how to explain technical security concepts in board language. The same principles apply to regulatory compliance:

- Avoid legal jargon. Instead of "We have implemented data subject access request workflows per Article 15," say "We can respond to customer data requests within the required timeframe."
- Frame compliance in business terms. Instead of "We achieved PCI-DSS Level 1 certification," say "We have validated that our payment systems meet card industry standards, protecting our ability to process transactions."
- Use analogies that boards already understand. For example, "Regulatory compliance is like financial auditing. We track obligations, maintain evidence, and demonstrate controls on demand."

Common Board Questions About Compliance (and How to Answer Them)

Directors ask predictable questions about compliance. The CISO who prepares answers in advance earns trust and efficiency.

"Are We Compliant?"

This is the most common question and the hardest to answer. Compliance is not binary; it is continuous.

Do not say "Yes" or "Mostly."

Say something like this: "We are compliant with current requirements in [list key regulations]. We have a structured process to monitor new obligations and absorb them within 90 days. Our last external audit confirmed no material gaps."

This answer acknowledges the complexity and demonstrates control.

"What Happens If We Are Not Compliant?"

Boards need to understand consequences in business terms, not legal abstractions.

You might say: "Non-compliance with GDPR could result in fines of up to four percent of global revenue, but the larger risk is reputational. Customers and partners expect us to protect their data. Non-compliance with SEC disclosure rules could trigger investor lawsuits and analyst downgrades. Non-compliance with the Payment Card Industry Data Security Standard, PCI-DSS, could mean we lose the ability to process credit card payments."

This frames compliance as risk management, which is a language boards speak fluently.

"How Fast Can We Adapt When Regulations Change?"

This is the question that separates mature organizations from reactive ones.

For example: "Our regulatory monitoring process flags new obligations within 30 days of passage. We assess impact within 60 days and implement required controls within 90 days. We track this as 'change velocity,' and we report it quarterly so you can see our adaptation tempo."

This answer demonstrates process, measurement, and transparency.

"What Is Our Exposure in [Specific Geography or Industry]?"

Directors often focus on markets or sectors where they see headline risk.

You might say: "For the EU, we are aligned with GDPR, and based on our business in California, we are aligned with CCPA and monitoring pending amendments. We have gap assessments underway for [state or region], and we will brief the board on any material exposure next quarter."

This shows you are thinking ahead and managing the portfolio of risk geographically.

Compliance Roadmap and Regulatory Adaptation

The board's expectation has evolved. They understand that the regulatory environment is complex, but they may not know where you fit in. That means you must brief them not only on today's compliance state but also on how you align with changes.

Building a System of Continuous Awareness

Directors assume that legal and regulatory monitoring is in place. What they value is how that awareness becomes action.

Outline your organization's "regulatory radar" in terms of both mechanism and cadence:

- Establish cadence: Tie regulatory landscape reviews to quarterly risk reviews.
- Define ownership: Legal spots it, compliance interprets it, security operationalizes it.
- Escalate to the board: Notify directors only when action requires governance approval, disclosure, or material shifts in exposure, resilience, or assurance.

Board framing: "We have institutionalized awareness. Every regulatory change hits an owner, a timeline, and a control update within 90 days."

Boards hear discipline, not bureaucracy.

What to Carry Forward

- Regulatory compliance is now a core element of board oversight. Directors are expected to understand the organization's obligations in data protection, cyber disclosure, and privacy, and to show that they exercised informed judgment.
- Your role is to present these requirements in a way that enables directors to ask the right questions, evaluate management's choices, and defend those decisions if challenged.
- When the company maintains a reliable process for monitoring regulatory changes, builds compliance expectations into its security program, and reports status with clarity and evidence, directors gain a clearer view of whether the organization is operating within its obligations.
- Compliance becomes a signal of governance strength rather than a source of uncertainty.

Chapter 7

Translating AI for the Board—Impact, Exposure, and Action

You are sitting in a quarterly board meeting. The chief innovation officer has just finished presenting your company's new AI strategy for agentic systems that will automate customer service, optimize pricing, and accelerate product development. Directors are nodding. Then the Audit Committee chair turns to you and asks:

"What could go wrong? What is our exposure? And how do we govern this?"

You have 10 minutes to help them understand a complex topic, but pre-alignment with your peers did not occur.

AI is no longer an innovation experiment. It is embedded in revenue systems, customer interactions, and operational decisions across your enterprise. The board's question is not whether to adopt AI, but whether they can govern it with the same rigor they apply to financial controls. Your role as CISO is to make AI risk visible, measurable, and governable.

The Governance Gap

Boards know how to govern financial systems, manufacturing processes, and customer data. They understand fiduciary duty, oversight mechanisms, and risk tolerance. They know how to ask: What decisions are we making? Who's accountable? How do we verify it's working?

But when AI enters the conversation, those questions often go unanswered. The chief information officer is deploying models to optimize operations. The chief technical officer is embedding AI into products. The chief innovation officer is racing to beat competitors. Meanwhile, the board is approving budgets without understanding what decisions they're delegating to algorithms, who's accountable when those algorithms fail, and how anyone knows if they're working as intended.

This is the governance gap: AI is making consequential business decisions, but the governance mechanisms boards rely on—clear ownership, documented processes, and regular assurance—have not caught up.

AI is not ungovernable. The problem is that most organizations are trying to govern it with technical controls rather than governance disciplines. Boards do not need to understand neural networks, training data, or model architectures. They need to answer the same three questions they ask about every other enterprise risk: Who decides? Who acts? and Who assures?

AI Governance in Three Questions

AI governance isn't about understanding models—it's about answering three questions:

1. What decisions is AI making?

Which business processes, customer interactions, and operational choices have been delegated to algorithms? What happens if those decisions are wrong? Where does human oversight still exist, and where has it been removed?

2. Who's accountable when it's wrong?

When an AI system makes a biased hiring decision, approves a fraudulent transaction, or generates misleading content, who owns the consequence? Is it the data scientist who built the model? The business leader who deployed it? The executive who approved the budget?

3. How do we know it's working?

Traditional monitoring assumes systems behave predictably. AI systems drift, degrade, and develop unexpected behaviors. How do you detect when a model stops working before it causes material harm? How do you prove to the board that your controls are effective?

These three questions, shown in Figure 7.1, map directly to how boards already govern enterprise risk. When you frame AI governance this way, directors recognize familiar territory. You are not asking them to learn a new discipline. You are helping them apply existing governance principles to a new technology.

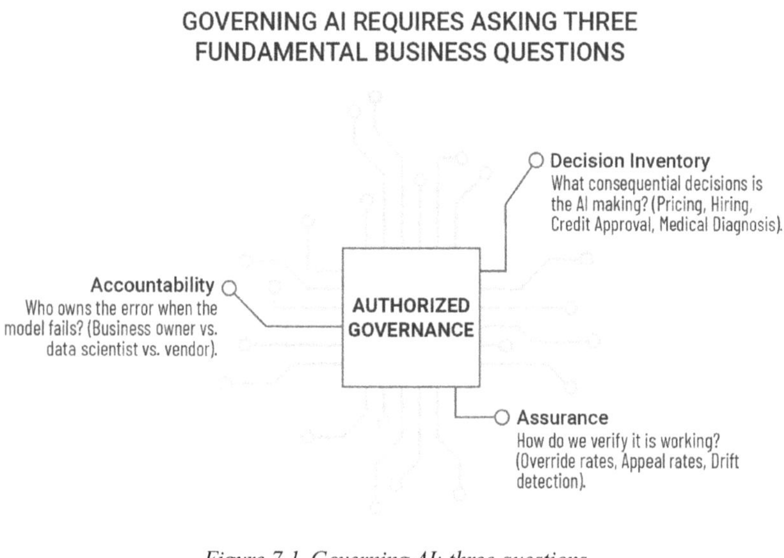

Figure 7.1. Governing AI: three questions

Question 1: What Decisions Is AI Making?

Boards need an inventory of consequential decisions being delegated to AI. Not a technical catalog of models, but a business inventory of where algorithms are making choices that affect revenue, customer trust, regulatory compliance, or operational continuity.

The failure to answer this question is what creates shadow AI risk. When business units deploy AI tools without central visibility, the organization loses track of what decisions are automated, what data those systems access, and what exposure they create.

Translating "What Decisions" for the Board

Most CISOs present AI risk as a technical problem. They talk about models, training data, and accuracy metrics. The board hears complexity but doesn't understand exposure.

Before (technical framing): "We have 47 AI models in production across the enterprise. Our data science team monitors model performance and retrains when accuracy degrades. We use a tiered approach based on NIST AI Risk Management Framework categories."

After (governance framing): "AI is currently making three categories of decisions that affect business outcomes:

- **Pricing decisions:** Our dynamic pricing model adjusts rates for 2,000 products daily, affecting approximately $4 million in daily revenue. If the model malfunctions, we could underprice inventory or price ourselves out of the market.
- **Credit approval:** Our lending model evaluates 15,000 applications per month. If it develops bias, we face regulatory penalties and reputational damage.

- **Customer service routing:** Our AI triages 50,000 support tickets monthly. If routing accuracy degrades, customer satisfaction drops and escalations increase.

Here's what each system decides, who owns each decision, and how we monitor for problems."

Why this works: The second version tells the board what they need to know to govern. They can see the business impact, understand the consequences of failure, and ask the right follow-up questions: "What's our tolerance for pricing errors? Who approves changes to the lending model? How do we know if customer satisfaction is declining because of routing failures?"

Question 2: Who's Accountable When It's Wrong?

AI creates accountability diffusion. When an algorithm makes a bad decision, responsibility spreads across multiple functions: the data scientists who built the model, the business leaders who deployed it, the IT team who operates it, and the executives who approved the budget. In traditional systems, accountability is clear. In AI systems, everyone has a piece of ownership, which often means no one has full ownership.

This diffusion creates governance risk. When something goes wrong—a biased hiring decision, a fraudulent approval, a customer harm—the board asks, "Who owns this?" If the answer is unclear, the board loses confidence in leadership's ability to govern AI effectively.

Your role as CISO is to make accountability explicit before incidents occur, not after.

Translating Accountability for the Board

Boards expect clear ownership. When you present AI governance, they need to see who owns decisions, who escalates problems, and who answers for failures.

Before (unclear accountability): "Our AI governance committee reviews high-risk models quarterly. We have a cross-functional working group with representatives from data science, engineering, legal, and business units. We follow a risk-based approach aligned with industry best practices."

After (clear accountability): "Every high-risk AI system has a named business owner accountable for outcomes. Here's how accountability works:

- **When our pricing AI recommends a discount that violates policy,** the VP of sales owns the decision to override or accept the recommendation. If the model consistently produces bad recommendations, the VP of sales escalates to the CIO for model review.
- **When our fraud model blocks a legitimate transaction,** customer service owns the recovery process with the affected customer. If false positives exceed our tolerance threshold, the VP of risk operations escalates for retraining.
- **When our hiring AI produces outcomes that raise fairness concerns,** the chief people officer owns the decision to pause, adjust, or discontinue use. Legal and compliance must approve any high-stakes deployment before it goes live.

Here's our accountability map showing who owns what when AI is involved."

Why this works: The second version gives the board specific people, specific decisions, and specific escalation paths. They can see governance in action, not just governance in theory.

The Six Ways AI Fails, and Who Owns Each Problem

When boards ask, "What could go wrong?" they need to understand the failure modes—model drift, bias propagation, hallucination, data poisoning, adversarial manipulation, and lack of operational transparency—and who's accountable for preventing or responding to each one:

Model drift

AI accuracy degrades because the data environment changed.
Accountability question: "Who monitors accuracy over time and decides when to retrain?"
Clear answer: "Data science monitors technical performance. The business owner decides if degradation requires action. Both escalate if the system falls below tolerance."

Bias propagation

Historical patterns in data encode unfairness that AI scales.
Accountability question: "Who tests for discrimination before deployment and who can halt a biased system?"
Clear answer: "Legal and compliance review fairness metrics before any high-stakes deployment. The business owner can pause or discontinue use. No system goes live without sign-off from both."

Hallucination

Generative AI produces convincing but false outputs.
Accountability question: "Who verifies AI-generated content before it reaches customers or regulators?"

Clear answer: "Business owners decide where generative AI can be used. Human verification is required before AI content reaches external stakeholders. IT logs what was generated vs. what was approved."

Data poisoning

Attackers manipulate training data to corrupt the model.
Accountability question: "Who protects training data and who validates its integrity?"
Clear answer: "Security protects data pipelines. Data teams validate training sets. Model owners test for unexpected behavior before deployment."

Adversarial manipulation

Attackers craft malicious inputs to trick the model.
Accountability question*:* "Who tests for adversarial resilience and who responds to exploitation?"
Clear answer: "Security conducts adversarial testing. Model owners implement input validation. Incident response includes AI-specific scenarios."

Lack of operational transparency

The AI system cannot explain how it reached its decision.
Accountability question: "Who ensures explainability for regulated decisions and who handles customer appeals?"
Clear answer: "Compliance must approve explainability for regulated decisions like credit or hiring. For other systems, the business owner decides if outcome monitoring is sufficient, with legal sign-off for high-risk deployments."

These accountability assignments prevent the "everyone's responsible, no one's accountable" problem that boards fear most.

Question 3: How Do We Know It's Working?

Traditional IT monitoring assumes systems behave predictably. Servers either run or crash. Applications either respond or time out. The failure modes are binary and observable.

AI systems fail differently. They degrade gradually. They develop biases over time. They produce wrong answers with complete confidence. They stop working correctly long before anyone notices.

This creates a detection problem: How do you know an AI system has stopped working when it's still running, still producing outputs, and still appearing functional?

Your role as CISO is to translate this detection challenge into assurance mechanisms the board can use to verify that AI governance is effective.

Translating Assurance for the Board

Boards need metrics that show whether AI systems are working as intended and whether governance mechanisms are detecting problems before they escalate.

Before (technical monitoring): "We monitor model accuracy, precision, recall, and F1 scores. Our MLOps platform tracks drift metrics and triggers alerts when performance degrades beyond baseline thresholds. We maintain model versioning and have rollback capabilities."

After (governance monitoring): "We track three metrics the board can use to assess AI governance effectiveness:

- **Override rate:** How often do humans override AI decisions? Rising override rates signal declining accuracy or trust. Current rate: 3.2% across all high-risk systems, within our 5% tolerance.

- **Appeal rate:** How many customers challenge AI decisions? Rising appeals signal fairness issues or poor explainability. Current rate: 1.8% of denials, stable over six months.
- **Detection speed:** How fast do we identify and fix problems? Current average: Problems detected within 72 hours, resolved within 14 days.

These metrics tell us whether our AI systems are maintaining quality and whether our governance is catching problems before they become incidents."

Why this works: The board can assess governance maturity without needing to understand technical details. Override rates, appeal rates, and detection speed are universal metrics that work across all AI systems and map to business outcomes.

Common Board Questions About AI (and How to Answer Them)

Even with strong translation, boards will ask challenging questions. Here's how to handle the most common ones:

"How do we know our AI isn't biased?"

Weak answer: "We use fairness metrics and regularly audit our models."

Strong answer: "We test for disparate impact before deployment and monitor outcomes by demographic group. Our 1.8% appeal rate tells us customers trust the system is fair."

Why it works: Specific example; shows monitoring in action; acknowledges perfect fairness is impossible, but demonstrates discipline.

"What happens if AI makes a decision that causes significant financial harm?"

Weak answer: "We have controls in place to help prevent that."

Strong answer: "Our pricing AI has three protection layers: 15% adjustment limit, daily VP review with override authority, and real-time anomaly alerts. Worst case, we revert to manual pricing within hours."

Why it works: Shows you've thought through the scenario; explains actual safeguards; demonstrates business and technical alignment.

"Isn't AI just a black box we can't control?"

Weak answer: "Modern explainable AI techniques allow us to understand model decisions."

Strong answer: "For high-stakes decisions like credit, we use explainable models. For lower-risk systems, we focus on governing outcomes—monitoring fairness, enabling overrides, and detecting problems quickly."

Why it works: Honest about limitations; reframes from technical explanation to governance outcomes; shows an appropriate risk-based approach.

"How much is this costing us?"

Weak answer: "AI governance requires investment in tools, audits, and staffing."

Strong answer: "AI governance costs about 8% of our total AI investment, roughly $400K annually. One regulatory penalty for bias could easily be double that number.

Why it works: Specific numbers, frames cost as risk management, and demonstrates business thinking.

"Do we need a separate AI committee, or can this stay with the Audit Committee?"

Weak answer: "That's a board composition decision."

Strong answer: "AI oversight can stay with audit or risk if they have the bandwidth. What matters is that someone at the board level asks the three governance questions regularly: What decisions is AI making? Who's accountable? How do we know it's working?"

Why it works: Gives the board flexibility; focuses on outcomes, not structure; shows you care about effective oversight, not organizational politics.

What Boards Need to Understand About AI Governance

When you translate AI governance for your board, focus on five key messages:

AI governance follows the same principles as financial governance.

You're not asking them to learn a new discipline. The same questions they ask about financial controls should be asked here. What are we deciding? Who owns it? How do we verify? These all apply to AI.

The board's role is oversight, not technical understanding.

They don't need to understand how models work. They need to confirm that management has clear ownership, monitoring, and an escalation plan for high-risk systems.

AI failures are often governance failures, not technical failures.

AI systems often don't fail due to their architectural design. They fail because no one asked the appropriate governance questions before building it. Technical expertise without governance discipline creates risk.

Not all AI carries the same risk.

A customer service routing AI and a credit approval AI have different stakes. Governance should be risk-based. The board should focus on high-autonomy, high-impact systems.

AI governance costs money, but prevents larger losses.

Investing 8–10% of AI budgets in governance prevents regulatory penalties, reputational damage, and failed deployments that could cost far more.

What to Carry Forward

- AI governance isn't about understanding neural networks or training algorithms. It's about answering three questions that the board already knows how to ask:
- **What decisions is AI making?**
  Translate technical systems into business decisions. Show the board where algorithms are making choices that affect revenue, customers, or compliance. Use business impact language, not model catalogs.
- **Who's accountable when it's wrong?**
  Make ownership explicit. Every high-risk system needs a business owner who's accountable for outcomes, with clear escalation paths when problems arise.
- **How do we know it's working?**
  Use governance metrics boards understand: override rates (Are humans trusting AI decisions?), appeal rates (Are customers challenging outcomes?), detection speed (How fast do we find and fix problems?).

- When you translate AI governance into these three questions, directors recognize familiar territory. They're not learning a new discipline—they're applying existing governance principles to emerging technology.
- Your role as CISO is to make AI risk visible, measurable, and governable. The board doesn't need to become AI experts. They need to see that you've extended the same governance rigor they expect for financial controls and operational processes.
- AI governance succeeds when the board can ask informed questions, evaluate your answers, and defend their oversight if challenged. That's not a technical capability. It's a governance discipline.

PART III

Execution & Authority

> *"The best way*
> *to predict the future*
> *is to create it."*
>
> — Peter Drucker

Chapter 8

Metrics That Matter to the Board

The quarterly board update reaches the metrics section. Three items are on screen:

- Critical systems can now recover in two hours, versus eight hours last quarter.
- 94 percent of revenue-generating applications have tested backup systems (up from 71 percent).
- Zero unplanned outages in customer-facing systems this quarter.

The audit chair nods. "This tells me something. I can see we're in better shape than three months ago." She flips back through her board packet. "The CFO showed operational uptime targets. Your recovery number lines up with what he needs. That's helpful."

That alignment did not happen by accident. Most cyber dashboards measure activity rather than outcomes. Boards do not need to know how many vulnerabilities were patched or how many alerts the SOC processed. They need to know where the business is exposed, how quickly operations can recover when something breaks, and whether they can trust the systems running the company.

This chapter provides a practical structure for selecting and presenting metrics that support board governance. It is simple by design. I call it the Board Cyber Metrics Framework, and it organizes metrics into three categories: exposure, resilience, and assurance.

Why Metrics Matter to Boards

Directors have three responsibilities when it comes to cyber risk:

- Understand where the organization is exposed
- Ensure it can recover from disruption
- Verify that leadership has visibility into the threat and control landscape

Metrics are the evidence that supports those duties.

Boards need metrics that show the following:

- Visibility into exposure: Which business capabilities are at risk, and why.
- Trend analysis: Whether we are getting better or worse over time.
- Governance focus: What needs board attention, and where management needs their authorization or alignment.

When metrics answer these questions, they become a governance tool.

The right metrics help boards govern. The wrong ones create confusion and erode trust.

Note: You may find that metrics are a kind of religion in your company, and that changing them is hard. If you are in this situation, start by introducing new metrics slowly. Show executives a comparison of old versus new measures. Showing value over time, rather than presenting a completely new page of reporting, will help you transition.

The Board Cyber Metrics Framework

The Board Cyber Metrics Framework, shown in Figure 8.1, organizes metrics into three categories that reflect how directors oversee risk. These categories are not new. They mirror how boards already govern financial performance and operational reliability across the organization. Using familiar mental models makes it easier for directors to understand what you are presenting.

Exposure

Exposure metrics show where the business is vulnerable. They identify which capabilities, services, or processes are at risk, and explain why.

- Residual risk of critical business services compared to tolerance
- Vendor dependency concentration that affects revenue or safety
- Data integrity exposure for financial or clinical systems
- Single points of failure in operational processes
- Third-party access to sensitive systems

Each exposure metric should follow a consistent pattern:

- Outcome at risk
- Exposure driver
- Impact range

For example, instead of reporting "10,200 vulnerable endpoints," present it like this:

"Payment processing systems have elevated exposure due to unpatched vulnerabilities in 40 percent of point-of-sale devices. Revenue at risk: approximately $2 million per day if systems go offline. Remediation timeline: 60 days."

Resilience

Resilience metrics show how quickly the organization can return to stable operation after a failure. They measure recovery performance and predictability.

- Actual recovery time versus target for critical services
- Containment time for material incidents over four quarters
- System failover performance for key processes
- Time to isolate compromised identities
- Vendor outage impact on core operations

Boards understand time and reliability. A resilience metric such as "Average recovery time for Tier 2 services: 8.4 hours (target: 10 hours)" tells a clear story. It shows performance, sets expectations, and highlights whether the organization is meeting its commitments.

Assurance

Assurance metrics show how confident leadership should be in the information they are using to evaluate posture. They reflect evidence quality and visibility.

- Severity and trend in closure of external audit findings
- High-risk exceptions: approved with secondary controls versus remediated
- Monitoring coverage for business-critical assets

- Testing cadence across tabletop, red team, and failover exercises
- Control validation results from independent assessments

Assurance metrics answer a vital question: Is our confidence justified?

If monitoring coverage for critical assets is 60 percent, the board knows they're exercising oversight with incomplete information. That is a governance issue, not just a technical one, and directors may need to adjust their risk appetite or insist on a remediation plan.

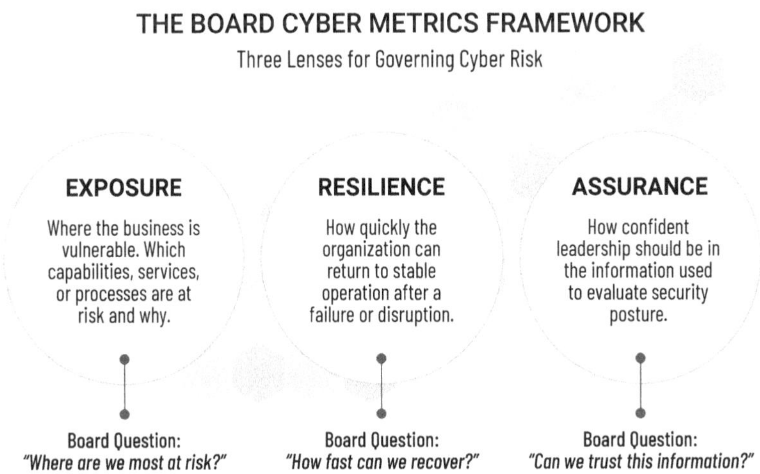

Figure 8.1. The Board Cyber Metrics Framework

Metrics Overload

A CISO at a financial services company presented 23 metrics to the board during a quarterly update. The dashboard included patch compliance rates, vulnerability counts by severity, mean time to detect and respond, security awareness training completion percentages, endpoint protection coverage, phishing simulation results, privileged access reviews, change management compliance, asset inventory accuracy, third-party risk assessments completed, penetration testing findings, security tool uptime, incident ticket volumes, false positive rates, threat intelligence alerts processed, and eight additional technical measures.

Each metric had a trend line, color coding, and comparison to industry benchmarks. The presentation took 25 minutes. Directors glazed over. Several checked their email. The audit chair interrupted, asking, "What do you actually need us to know?"

The CISO couldn't answer clearly. Too much data, no hierarchy of what mattered most.

What the CISO Did Differently

Next quarter, the CISO condensed to six metrics organized by exposure (residual risk vs. tolerance), resilience (recovery time vs. targets), and assurance (audit findings and remediation status). Board engagement improved immediately. The same audit chair said, "Now I can see where we stand."

What This Teaches

Boards don't want comprehensive dashboards—they want governance-ready insights. More metrics don't equal better governance. They create noise that obscures signal.

Organize around principles boards already understand: Where are we exposed? How quickly can we recover? How confident should we be? Keep the count low (six to eight metrics maximum), show trends over time, and connect each metric to business outcomes. If you can't explain in one sentence why a metric matters to board oversight, cut it.

The lesson: Less is more. Clarity beats comprehensiveness.

When Boards Ask: "What's the Dollar Amount?"

Directors sometimes ask for quantification of cyber risk: "What's our exposure in dollars?" or "What's the ROI on this security investment?" These are reasonable governance questions, but precise quantification of cyber risk is harder than it appears.

Quantification works well in the following circumstances:

- Comparing defined risks (ransomware recovery cost vs. data breach notification cost)
- Justifying specific investments (cost of new control vs. estimated loss reduction)
- Meeting regulatory requirements that demand financial risk assessment

Quantification becomes misleading when:

- Predicting unknown attack vectors or novel threats
- Estimating reputational damage (impossible to model accurately)
- Measuring systemic risks like supply chain compromise or nation-state attacks

Here's the practical approach this book recommends:

Work with the CFO; don't quantify in isolation.

Financial risk quantification is the CFO's domain. When boards ask for dollar amounts, this is your opportunity to demonstrate executive alignment, not technical expertise. Schedule time with the CFO or finance team before the board meeting. Walk through your risk scenarios together. Let them apply to the organization's financial methodology the same frameworks they use for operational, market, and strategic risk. When you present to the board, you and the CFO speak the same language because you built the assessment together.

Use ranges, not point estimates.

Say "$4 to 5 million potential exposure" rather than "$4.3 million." Ranges acknowledge uncertainty while still providing context. Your CFO will appreciate this, as they understand that false precision undermines credibility.

Use scenarios rather than predictions.

"If ransomware takes down our core systems, recovery costs $X to $Y based on downtime duration. Here's our current recovery capability." The CFO can help translate downtime into revenue impact using models that finance already maintains.

Focus on relative priority.

"This risk is higher than that risk because..." Boards need to know where to allocate resources, not exact dollar precision. Finance teams excel at portfolio prioritization; leverage their expertise.

Be transparent about uncertainty.

When boards press for precision you cannot provide, explain why: "The honest answer is that we cannot quantify this with confidence. Here's what we know, here's what we don't know, and here's how we're managing the uncertainty." The CFO will respect this candor more than manufactured precision.

This governance-focused approach, aligned with exposure, resilience, and assurance, works better for most boards than complex statistical models built in isolation. It provides the clarity directors need without creating false precision that undermines credibility. Advanced quantification methodologies exist and have value in specific regulatory contexts, but most boards respond best to clear risk scenarios, ranges, and relative prioritization developed collaboratively with finance. That's what this book teaches you to deliver.

Note: Methodologies like FAIR (factor analysis of information risk) enable CISOs to quantify risk using probability distributions and dollar ranges. When done well, this gives boards the financial language they're accustomed to. But FAIR cannot be adopted in a vacuum. Before implementing any quantitative risk methodology, the board and executive team must align on foundational questions, such as: What loss scenarios matter most? What probability threshold triggers action? What financial impact is "material" for this organization? Without that alignment, FAIR produces rigorous math that no one acts on.

Selecting Board-Ready Metrics

Not every metric belongs in the boardroom. The best board metrics share four characteristics: they're business-aligned, stable over time, actionable, and minimal.

Business-aligned

The metric must connect to business outcomes.
Business-aligned: "Residual risk for payment processing compared to tolerance."
Not board-ready on its own: "Number of critical CVEs."

Stable over time

Boards need consistency to track trends. Changing metrics every quarter forces directors to relearn the dashboard instead of evaluating progress.

Actionable

The metric should indicate if the program is on track. If the board cannot use it to govern, it does not belong in the packet.

Minimal

You can use a simple test for any proposed board metric:

- Does it clearly relate to a business outcome?
- Does it fit into exposure, resilience, or assurance categories?
- Can we show at least four quarters of trend data?
- Can we explain it in one sentence without technical jargon?

If the answer is no to any of these, reconsider including it.

Six Board Metric Examples

Here is a starting point that works across industries:

- Critical services with required controls in place (exposure): Shows where exposure exists in revenue-driven systems.
- Recovery time vs. target for critical services (resilience): Demonstrates operational readiness.
- High-risk vendors with mitigation controls (exposure and resilience): Highlights third-party risk and how you are managing it.
- Material incidents over four quarters (resilience): Shows whether the program is improving.
- External audit findings and remediation status (assurance): Reflects regulatory compliance and control validation.
- Progress on strategic cyber initiatives (assurance): Connects

security investments to business priorities, for example, progress on a multi-year initiative to enable new digital revenue.

These six metrics give the board visibility into exposure, resilience, and assurance. They are stable, business-aligned, and actionable.

Presenting Metrics Effectively

Data without context is just numbers. Boards need narrative, trends, and clear takeaways to interpret metrics.

Use Simple Visualizations

A trend line showing incident containment time over four quarters tells a story. Use simple, clean visuals:

- Line charts for trends
- Bar charts for comparisons
- Heat maps for risk concentration

Aim for a one-page view where the most critical information is visible at a glance. Later in this chapter, in The One-Page Metrics View, we will bring these ideas together into a one-page layout you can drop directly into your board pack.

Provide Context and Narrative

Every metric needs three elements:

- What it shows: "This metric tracks recovery time for services that support online banking."

- Why it matters: "Faster recovery reduces revenue loss and customer impact."
- What changed: "Recovery time improved by 15 percent this quarter due to enhanced runbooks."

Context turns data into insight. Without it, boards are left guessing.

Highlight Trends, Not Snapshots

A single data point does not tell the board whether things are getting better or worse. Show trends over time, ideally four quarters, so directors can see trajectory and momentum.

For example, instead of "12 high-risk exceptions this quarter," show:

"High-risk exceptions over the last four quarters: 18, 15, 12, 12. Trend: improving, but the plateau suggests we may need a process review."

Common Metrics Mistakes to Avoid

There are several things to avoid when it comes to metrics:

Metrics overload

More metrics do not mean better governance. They mean confusion. Boards cannot effectively track 20 metrics. Stick to roughly six core metrics and keep them consistent over time.

Vanity metrics

Vanity metrics make the program look busy, but they don't support governance. Examples:

- "Blocked 10 million phishing emails" (expected activity, not risk reduction)

- "Deployed advanced SOC use cases" (activity, not outcome)
- "Achieved 99 percent patching compliance" (technical measure, not business impact)

Vanity metrics create false confidence. Focus on metrics that show exposure, resilience, and assurance. Ask of every metric: "Would this still look good if our actual risk posture were getting worse?"

If the answer is yes, it is likely a vanity metric.

Technical jargon

If a metric requires technical translation in the meeting, it does not belong in the boardroom in its raw form.

Technical: "Mean time to detect (MTTD) decreased from 72 hours to 48 hours."

Board-ready: "We now identify security incidents 33 percent faster, which reduces potential data loss."

Stoplight grids without context

Red, yellow, and green indicators are meaningless without explanation. What does "yellow" mean? Who decided on that threshold? What changes when it becomes red?

Stoplight grids oversimplify risk and hide nuance. Use them sparingly, and only with clear definitions and supporting narrative. Many boards do better without them at all.

Metrics Maturity and Evolution

Metrics should evolve as the program matures. Early-stage programs focus on foundational metrics to build capabilities and close critical gaps. Mature programs shift to strategic metrics to enable growth and stay ahead of threats.

Stage 1: Foundational metrics

- Control implementation progress
- Critical vulnerability remediation timelines
- Incident response readiness (for example, tabletop exercise completion)

Stage 2: Operational metrics

- Recovery time performance
- Incident containment time
- Audit finding remediation status

Stage 3: Strategic metrics

- Residual risk compared to tolerance
- Security program contribution to business enablement or strategic initiatives
- Threat intelligence integration and proactive defense indicators

As the program matures, metrics should shift from measuring activity to measuring outcomes.

The board's questions change from "Are we doing the basics?" to "Are we managing risk effectively?" Metrics should reflect that evolution.

Foundational and operational metrics do not disappear. They move to management dashboards. The board's view becomes more strategic, while operational teams still track implementation details.

Good Versus Bad Metrics Presentations

Let's see what it looks like to present poorly, followed by an effective example, using the Board Cyber Metrics Framework.

The Bad Example

A CISO presents the following metrics to the board:

- 87 percent patching compliance
- 2.3 million security incident and event management (SIEM) events processed
- 15 new security tools deployed
- 99.7 percent email security effectiveness

Why this fails:

- These are activity metrics, not risk metrics.
- There is no business context or impact.
- There are no trends in the data.
- The language is technical and full of jargon.
- Several numbers qualify as vanity metrics.

None of these metrics tells the board whether customer-facing services are more at risk than they were last quarter.

The board's reaction: silence, confusion, and a loss of confidence in the CISO's ability to communicate risk.

The Good Example

The same CISO revises the presentation using the Board Cyber Metrics Framework.

- **Exposure:** "Enterprise resource planning (ERP) systems: residual risk is elevated due to staffing gaps in patching and support. Estimated revenue at risk: $1 million per day. Mitigation is in progress; completion target is 30 days."

- **Resilience:** "Recovery time for Tier 3 services: 18 hours versus a target of 24 hours. Performance has been stable over the last four quarters."
- **Assurance:** "External audit findings: two high-severity findings, down from five last quarter. Remediation plan is on track, and one of the two findings is already closed."

Why this works:

- Metrics are business-aligned and anchored in exposure, resilience, and assurance, with clear context and trends.
- Governance implications are explicit: Monitor recovery performance and validate remediation progress.
- There is no unnecessary technical jargon or vanity counting.

In practice, you would present a small handful of metrics in each category. This example focuses on the style and content of board-ready metrics.

The One-Page Metrics View

Boards often have a lot of material to review. A one-page metrics view ensures they see the most critical information immediately. It brings together the principles in this chapter, minimal and business-aligned, into a single layout you can reuse every quarter.

- Row 1: Exposure—where we are most at risk.
- Row 2: Resilience—how quickly we can recover.
- Row 3: Assurance—how confident we can be.

Row 1: Exposure

Top three business services with elevated residual risk.

Short explanation of the exposure driver for each.

Keep each explanation to a single sentence that names the cause and direction of change. For example:

"Customer onboarding, higher exposure this quarter due to single-region data center and growing volume."

Row 2: Resilience

Actual versus target recovery time for top services.

Notable vendor or infrastructure dependencies.

Use a standard unit, such as hours, to restore top services after a major incident, so the board can compare resilience levels across the portfolio. Where possible, show quarter-over-quarter trends, not just a point-in-time number.

Row 3: Assurance

Severity and trend of audit findings.

High-risk exception trend.

Show trends over at least four quarters so directors can see whether remediation efforts are working. Be clear about the scope, for example, external audits only, or both internal and external.

Over time, use the same one-page view every quarter. The specific metrics within each row may evolve as your program matures, but the structure should stay stable. Directors learn where to look for exposure and how to interpret trends.

See Figure 8.2 for an example.

THE ONE-PAGE METRICS VIEW: GOVERNANCE AT A GLANCE

EXPOSURE

Top 3 business services with elevated risk and their exposure drivers.
Ex. Customer onboarding: higher expusure this quarter due to single-region data center.

1. ....
2. ....
3. ....

RESILIENCE

Actual vs. target recovery time for top services (with trend).

Example see graph:

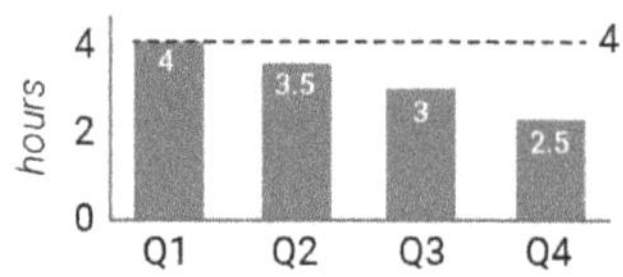

ASSURANCE

Severity and trend of audit findings (internal/external).

Example see graph:

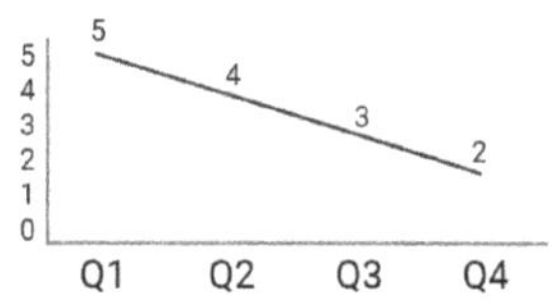

MOVEMENT AND DECISIONS

What Improved:
Recovery times for Tier 2 services are now 15% ahead of target.

What Degraded:
Residual risk for ERP systems increased due to new vulnerabilities.

Figure 8.2. The one-page metrics view

What to Carry Forward

- Metrics are evidence, not the story. Directors need to understand where the business is exposed, how well it can recover from disruption, and how confident leadership is in its assessment.
- Do not create metrics in a silo. The board metrics are not for you; they package your message in an easy-to-read format for the board.
- The Board Cyber Metrics Framework provides a straightforward way to communicate those signals without technical noise.
- When you use this structure consistently, metrics become a source of alignment rather than confusion. They enable the board to govern risk with confidence and build trust with the CISO.

Chapter 9

Presenting to the Board

The text came in at 4:55 p.m. on a Tuesday.

"Board wants cyber update tomorrow. Audit committee, 9 am on the incident from last week."

A vendor portal exposed metadata for six hours before your team caught it. No customer impacts. No data exfiltration. Clean containment. But the board did not know that yet. All they knew was "breach" and "vendor."

You had sixteen hours.

Preparation

That night, you built the deck and sent it to the CEO at 11 p.m.:

"Ready to walk through this in the morning if helpful."

The reply came at 6 a.m.:

"Looks good. Keep it tight. They'll have questions."

In the Room

At 9:02 a.m., you stood at the end of the conference table. Seven directors. The audit chair opened:

"Walk us through what happened and what it means."

Seven minutes. Four slides. No jargon. You started with the outcome:

"We identified and contained an exposure in a vendor portal within six hours. No customer data was accessed. No business operations were affected. We have completed the root cause review and implemented three controls to prevent recurrence."

Then you walked backward: what triggered the detection, how containment worked, and what the vendor did wrong. You closed with the path forward:

"The vendor relationship continues under enhanced monitoring. We will confirm final control implementation within 30 days."

The Questions That Matter

Silence. Then the audit chair:

"Six hours from detection to containment?"

"Correct."

"And you are confident no data left the environment?"

"We validated that through log review and third-party forensics. The evidence is in the appendix."

She nodded. The CFO leaned forward:

"What is our disclosure obligation?"

"We briefed general counsel immediately. This does not meet materiality thresholds under our framework. General counsel confirmed no SEC filing is required."

The CFO sat back. The audit chair looked at you.

"Thank you."

You were out of the room by 9:14.

Takeaway: Why the Presentation Worked

That presentation worked because you built it around their questions, not your expertise. You gave them the outcome first, the evidence second, and the path forward third. You did not apologize. You did not over-explain. You translated a technical event into a governance answer.

The four slides:

1. Executive summary with outcome and business impact
2. Timeline showing detection to containment in six hours
3. Root cause and three controls implemented
4. Vendor status and 30-day confirmation milestone

The Purpose of the Board Presentation

Board presentations serve one function: enabling effective governance. Every slide, sentence, and visual either builds confidence in management or introduces uncertainty.

The measure of success is not applause. It is that directors leave the room knowing what changed, what you are doing about it, and what they are accountable for.

Preparing for Board Meetings

Preparation separates effective board communicators from technical briefers. The board expects you to arrive with a straightforward narrative, aligned messaging, and answers already coordinated with the CEO and general counsel.

The 72-Hour Rule

Use a simple preparation timeline (Table 9.1).

Timing	Action	Purpose
3 days prior	Finalize narrative and align with executive team	Unified messaging; assign question handlers
2 days prior	Distribute advance materials	Give directors time to review; surface concerns early
1 day prior	Conduct dry run with team	Full rehearsal with timing; test difficult questions
Day of meeting	Arrive early; display summary slide	Professional presence; set tone

Alignment Brief (Three Days Prior)

Schedule 30 minutes with the CEO, CFO, and general counsel. Walk through the following:

- Cross-deck data validation: confirm your numbers match what the CFO or CEO will present.
- Question assignments: who owns technical questions, who owns financial, who owns legal.

This brief prevents contradictions in the room. If the CFO says, "incident costs were $400,000," and you say "$350,000," the directors notice. Alignment builds credibility.

Rehearsal (One Day Prior)

Run through the entire presentation with your team. Time it: about one minute opening, six minutes core content, two minutes to support an approval (if any), and one minute close.

Practice answering the three questions you least want to hear.

Structuring Your Content

Every effective board presentation follows the same sequence:

1. **Situation:** What changed since the last meeting
2. **Significance:** Why it matters to the business
3. **Status:** What is being done and what remains
4. **Support:** What you need from the board, whether awareness, discussion, or approval

Directors absorb information faster when the structure is simple and consistent.

Example: Presenting a Ransomware Tabletop Exercise

Weak structure:
"We conducted a ransomware drill last quarter. Twelve executives participated; here are the findings…"

Strong structure:

- **Situation:** "We ran a simulated ransomware attack to test our ability to recover critical operations within 48 hours."
- **Significance:** "The exercise revealed two dependencies in the human resource information system that would delay recovery by 36 hours, putting Q4 employee payments at risk."
- **Status:** "We have addressed one dependency through redundant routing. The second requires vendor architecture changes, which are in progress."
- **Support:** "This is for awareness. We will confirm completion at the next quarterly update."

The second structure gives the board clear understanding of your message. They know what happened, why it matters, what you are doing, and what they need to do (in this case, nothing other than tracking progress).

Frame each section with the board's perspective in mind.

The Importance of Headlines

The first conclusion a director makes about your slide is whether it matters. That judgment happens in roughly two seconds, before you speak. The slide title drives that judgment.

Most slides are titled by category: "Metrics." "Vulnerabilities." "Program Update." These titles tell the board nothing. They signal reporting, not relevance. Headlines transform passive titles into active claims.

Why Headlines Matter

When you use headlines:

- You guide the conversation with a clear point of view.
- You demonstrate executive presence. Synthesis is leadership.
- You prepare the board for the right questions.

The difference:

Weak: "Metrics in Q2."
Strong: "Resilience improving, but two dependencies still create concentrated exposure."

The strong version anchors the board in meaning immediately. They understand the message before you explain the data.

Weak Titles to Strong Headlines

Use these as patterns:

Weak: "Q4 metrics"
Strong: "Resilience posture improving; two dependencies remain under active management."

Weak: "Critical vulnerabilities"
Strong: "The system dependencies driving our highest-impact exposure"

Weak: "Threat landscape"
Strong: "How attacker behavior is shifting toward identity-based disruption"

Weak: "Cyber incidents"
Strong: "The five actions that will reduce our exposure curve most over the next six months"

Notice the structure: every strong headline contains an outcome, a driver, and an implication.

The Headline Formula

Headline = Outcome + Driver + Implication

- **Outcome:** The net effect directors need to know
- **Driver:** What is causing that effect
- **Implication:** Why it matters to the business or board

Example: "Resilience improving, but payment concentration keeps exposure elevated"

See Figure 9.1 for an at-a-glance view. Condense to eight to twelve words. Make it scannable. Make it decisive.

Figure 9.1. The headline formula

How the Board Consumes Information

You have roughly seven to ten minutes of board attention. It may be less if the agenda is packed. Directors arrive with thick packets that they likely skimmed on the flight in.

Your presentation must work on three levels:

- **Scannable:** A director skimming slides while you speak should still understand the message.
- **Verbal:** Your spoken narrative should stand on its own without the slides.
- **Standalone:** If a director reads the deck later without you, the conclusion should still be obvious.

Follow these design principles:

- Lead with the conclusion, not chronology. Start with the answer, then show supporting evidence.

- Use space deliberately. One clear idea beats twelve data points.
- Make every element relevant. If removing a chart would not change understanding, remove it.

Consider your in-room presence:

Arrive ten minutes early. Bring one note card with your opening, close, and ask.
Stand if the room allows. Make eye contact. Use declarative sentences. Avoid filler words.
Most importantly, listen actively. If a director asks a question mid-presentation, answer it immediately. Do not defer to a future slide.

Handling Q&A and Difficult Conversations

Slides build confidence. Q&A tests it. Many directors judge the CISO less by the slides and more by the five minutes of dialogue that follow.

Follow these ground rules:

- Pause before answering. A two-second pause signals you are thinking, not reacting.
- Reframe to confirm scope: "To clarify, you are asking about vendor exposure specifically, not internal controls?"
- Lead with the outcome. Give the answer first, then the supporting detail.
- Use business language. Avoid jargon unless the director uses it first.
- Admit unknowns confidently: "I do not have that data in front of me, but I will confirm and send it by the end of the day."

Response Pattern: Answer, Assurance, Next Step

Example:

Director: "Was customer data exposed in the incident?"

You:

- **Answer:** "No. We confirmed that no data left the environment."
- **Assurance:** "We validated this through log review and third-party forensics within 12 hours of detection."
- **Next step:** "The full forensics report is in the appendix, and I can walk you through the methodology after the meeting if helpful."

This structure gives the director what they need: the fact, confidence in the fact, and an option for deeper detail.

When a Director Challenges Your Framing

Sometimes a director will reframe your message in a way that shifts the tone. This often happens when they are testing your composure or are genuinely concerned.

Director: "So what you are saying is we are vulnerable."

You: "What I am saying is we have residual risk in this area, which is within our stated risk appetite. We are actively managing it through compensating controls and targeted investments. The trajectory is toward lower exposure, and we will report progress quarterly."

You did not say "no, you are wrong." You reframed the issue in terms the board uses to govern.

Ambush Questions

Occasionally, a director will ask a question designed to surface accountability gaps.

Director: "Why were we not told about this sooner?"

This question has two layers: the factual answer (when you notified them) and the implied criticism (you should have known earlier). Address both.

You: "We notified the audit chair within 24 hours of confirming the issue met our materiality threshold. I agree that timeliness is critical, which is why we have strengthened our escalation criteria to surface issues earlier in the assessment process. The updated framework went into effect last month, and we will report on its effectiveness at the next meeting."

You acknowledged the concern, took ownership of the improvement, and closed the loop. That is how you turn criticism into confidence.

What to Carry Forward

- A great board presentation is not about showing your technical depth. It is about making governance easier. In seven to ten minutes, lead with the outcome, explain why it matters to the business, and close with a clear ask, using simple headlines, one-idea visuals, and a tight narrative built around situation, significance, status, and support.
- Headlines will change your slides from a standard update to a slide that grabs attention and makes your audience put their phones down.
- When you prepare with the CEO and general counsel, rehearse your story, and handle Q&A with calm, outcome-first answers, you stop being a technical briefer and become a trusted advisor the board relies on.

Chapter 10

Crisis Communication

The call came at 2:47 a.m. Unauthorized access detected in a supplier gateway. You know from the location that customer data could be exposed. The incident response team is already mobilizing, but you know that the next 12 hours will be defined not only by technical containment, but also by communication.

By 6:00 a.m., three executives will need a briefing. By 9:00 a.m., the board chair will expect clarity. By noon, the Audit Committee may convene. The technical response will follow established playbooks. The board communication requires something different: the ability to replace anxiety with structure while the facts are still moving.

This is the reality of crisis communication. Boards are designed to be cautious, analytical, and primed for control. When volatility arrives, that instinct intensifies. Conversations compress. Risk appetite vanishes. Your work stops being informational and becomes emotional governance.

Your job is to demonstrate that the organization remains in control. That every action, every update, and every silence is chosen, not accidental. This is the core discipline of board communication under stress: replacing randomness with structure and rhythm.

Directors can manage bad news. They cannot manage randomness.

Your cadence, tone, and phrasing become visible proof that leadership remains intentional even when certainty has vanished. In those moments, information loses value if it lacks sequence. Your task is to restore order and give the board a steady sense that someone is deliberately choosing the next move.

What the Board Is Really Evaluating

During a crisis, every message must answer three silent board questions:

- Are they seeing clearly? (Awareness)
- Are they acting deliberately? (Control)
- Are they communicating predictably? (Discipline)

When those three signals are visible, confidence returns. When they are not, governance instincts take over, and the board starts managing in your place.

Crisis communication is not about concluding an incident. It is about preserving trust while the facts are still moving.

Let me be direct. You will not have everything perfectly prepared. You will be improvising more than you would like. The situation will be messier than any tabletop exercise. But if you consistently demonstrate these three signals, the board will trust you to lead through the crisis.

Before the Crisis: Preparation That Actually Helps

Most CISOs invest heavily in technical incident response capabilities and far less in crisis communication readiness. Yet when a major incident occurs, communication failures often cause more board-level damage than the technical incident itself.

A board can work through a breach with you. They cannot tolerate being blindsided, contradicted, or left in the dark.

A wise mentor once told me: The only thing worse than bad news, is bad news late.

You do not need an elaborate crisis communication infrastructure. You need five essentials: contact information, escalation criteria, a message framework, alignment with the CEO and general counsel, and one practice session per year.

Current Board Contact Information

Common roles you should have up-to-date contact info for include the following:

- Board chair
- Audit committee chair
- CEO
- General counsel

Verify these contacts quarterly. Test them during tabletops and at least annually with a brief message.

During a crisis, you cannot be hunting for phone numbers or wondering if an email address still works.

There are tools that manage contact trees. They can help, but only if you have done the work to obtain accurate information and keep it up to date.

Clear Escalation Criteria

When do you notify the board?

You need clear thresholds, agreed in advance with your CEO and board. Here is a simple framework.

Notify immediately if any of these are true:

- Customer data potentially exposed.
- Critical systems down for more than four hours.
- Regulatory notification is likely required.
- Probable media coverage.
- Potential direct cost or revenue impact over $1 million.

Notify within four hours if:

- Significant security incident contained, but impacts are still being assessed.
- Potential but unconfirmed customer impact.
- Attacker activity detected and contained.

Include in the next scheduled update if:

- Routine security incidents with no business impact.
- Attempted attacks that were blocked.

Do not overcomplicate this. When in doubt, notify. Early notification with "this may be less serious than initially assessed" is far better than late notification with "it turned out to be serious."

A Simple Message Framework

You do not need elaborate templates. You need a simple structure you can remember at 3 a.m.

Three-part crisis update:

- What we know (confirmed facts only).

- What we are doing (containment, investigation, and recovery actions).
- When you will hear next (specific time for the next update).

That is it. This structure works verbally or in writing. It works for the first notification and every update after. It keeps you focused on what matters.

Unity with the CEO and General Counsel

Before any crisis hits, you need agreement with your CEO and general counsel on three things:

- Who speaks to the board: usually you for technical matters, but sometimes the CEO leads.
- How you will align: a quick sync before board communication, even if it is only five minutes.
- What consistency means: same facts, same severity assessment, same timeline.

Fragmented executive communication can quickly destroy board confidence. If the CEO says, "We believe customer data was not accessed," and you say, "We are still investigating whether data was accessed," the board will question whether anyone is in control.

Plan now for how you will stay aligned when things are moving fast.

One Practice Session per Year

You do not need quarterly tabletops with elaborate scenarios. You need one annual session where you practice delivering bad news to your board.

How to do this:

- Select a realistic scenario (for example, ransomware, data breach, supplier compromise).
- Deliver a crisis briefing to your audit committee as if it is real.
- Ask them to push with hard, skeptical questions.
- Debrief as a group: what worked, what did not, what you would do differently.

This builds muscle memory for high-pressure communication and reduces board anxiety when a real crisis hits.

That is the preparation that helps. Everything else is nice to have but not essential. If you have these five elements in place, you are ahead of most organizations.

During the Crisis: What to Say When You Do Not Have All the Answers

The hardest part of crisis communication is managing uncertainty. You do not have all the answers. The situation is changing rapidly. The board is understandably anxious.

Here is how to communicate effectively despite incomplete information.

Lead with What You Know, Acknowledge What You Do Not

Structure every crisis update in three parts.

1. What we know (confirmed facts only)

Be conservative about what you claim to "know." These are facts verified by multiple sources or forensic evidence.

- We detected unauthorized access at 2:47 a.m.
- The access was to our supplier gateway environment.
- We have isolated the affected system.
- External forensics are on-site.

2. What we are doing (deliberate actions)

   These are the containment, investigation, and recovery actions you are taking right now.
   - We have isolated the affected system to prevent lateral movement.
   - We have engaged an external forensics firm to conduct analysis.
   - We have reset all credentials for the affected environment.
   - We are coordinating with legal on disclosure obligations.

3. When you will hear next

   Give the board a specific time for your next update. This is critical.
   - I will update you again at 4:00 p.m. or sooner if the situation changes materially.
   - If you do not hear from me before then, it means the situation is stable and we are continuing the investigation as planned.

This structure gives the board confidence that you are seeing clearly (what you know), acting deliberately (what you are doing), and communicating predictably (the timeline for the next update).

Maintain Cadence: Set Clear Expectations for Updates

One of the most effective ways to reduce board anxiety during a crisis is to set clear expectations for when you will provide updates.

What to say:

I will update you again at [specific time] or sooner if the situation changes materially. If you do not hear from me before then, it means the situation is stable and we are continuing the investigation as planned.

Why this works:

- Gives the board a predictable rhythm, which reduces anxiety
- Prevents ad hoc requests that distract from the response
- Signals that you are in control of the communication process
- Allows you to focus on incident response without constant interruption

If you miss a committed update time, send a brief message:

Update delayed due to ongoing forensic analysis. No material changes in the situation. Revised update time: 8:00 p.m.

Delays are understood. Silence is not.

Language Discipline: Words That Signal Control

Word choice sets the tone for crisis posture. Boards hear verbs before they hear context.

Preferred Language

Use language that signals awareness, control, and progress.

Use these:

- Detected (shows awareness)

- Contained (shows control)
- Isolated (shows deliberate action)
- Verified (shows thoroughness)
- Stabilized (shows progress)

Avoid or qualify these:

- Breach (use "unauthorized access" until regulatory definitions apply)
- Loss (use "exposure" until loss is confirmed)
- Secure (use "protected" or "controlled")
- Resolved (use "contained" until forensics is complete)
- Safe (use "stable" or "within tolerance")

Replace Speculation with Evidence

Before you speak, run your language through this filter. The pattern is consistent: acknowledge the question, provide what you know, and commit to a timeline for what you do not know.

Do not say: "We think customer data was not accessed."
Say: "Current evidence shows no data exfiltration. Forensics will confirm by 6:00 p.m."

Do not say: "We hope to have systems back online soon."
Say: "System restoration is underway. We expect completion by midnight."

Do not say: "We believe the threat is contained."
Say: "Containment measures are in place and holding. We are monitoring for any additional activity."

Do not say: "Everything is under control."
Say: "We have specific containment measures in place, and our incident response team is fully mobilized."

Precision creates credibility. Overstatement erodes it.

Before and After Examples

Scenario: Board member asks, "How did this happen?"
Weak response: "We think someone clicked on a phishing email, but we are not sure yet."
Strong response: "Root cause analysis is underway. Current evidence points to compromised supplier credentials. We will have confirmed findings in our after-action review by [date]."

Scenario: Board member asks, "Are we going to be in the news?"
Weak response: "I do not think so. It is not that bad."
Strong response: "Based on current evidence, no customer data is compromised, there is no operational disruption, and no regulatory notification is required. I do not expect this to become public. However, we are coordinating with communications and legal to prepare for any scenario. If that assessment changes, I will notify you immediately."

Scenario: Board member asks, "Could this happen again?"
Weak response: "You can never guarantee; attackers are sophisticated, we will do our best."
Strong response: "We are implementing immediate containment measures and will conduct a full control review. Systemic improvements will be prioritized in our after-action plan. I will present specific enhancements to the audit committee within 30 days."

Unity: Operating as One Voice

Crisis communication only works when the CISO, CEO, and general counsel operate as one voice. Misalignment reads as confusion, and confusion erodes confidence faster than the incident itself.

Before any board communication, you need a quick sync, even five minutes, to align on three things:

- Facts: what you know with certainty, what you are still investigating, and your confidence level.
- Framing: how you will describe the event, the severity level, and the business impact.
- Next steps: what actions management is taking, what you need from the board, and the timeline.

Example of good unity:

Board member: "Should we pay the ransom?"

CEO: "That requires board input before we can move forward. [CISO] will brief us on the technical situation. [GC] will brief us on the legal considerations. Then I will share my recommendation."
CISO: "We have backups for all affected systems. We can restore operations without paying. Restoration will take eight hours. We can recover without paying a ransom."
General counsel: "Paying a ransom may violate sanctions if the attacker is a sanctioned entity. It also does not guarantee data deletion. From a legal perspective, I advise against payment."
CEO: "Based on technical and legal input, I recommend we do not pay. We restore from backups. The cost is eight hours of downtime and approximately $150,000 in restoration costs,

which is less than the ransom demand and avoids legal risk. Do you agree?"

This is unity: three executives, one coherent narrative, and a clear recommendation.

When Capital One disclosed its 2019 breach, the public communication reflected this kind of coordination. Within ten days of discovering the unauthorized access, the company synchronized its public announcement with the FBI's arrest of the individual responsible. The CEO issued a direct statement that took personal accountability without hedging or deflecting. Customer remediation, including two years of free credit monitoring, was announced alongside the disclosure, not weeks later. No crisis response is flawless, and Capital One faced significant scrutiny over the underlying vulnerability that enabled the breach. But the post-discovery communication demonstrated what disciplined coordination between technical, legal, and executive teams produces: a coherent narrative delivered on a deliberate timeline.

Example of poor unity:

Board member: "Is customer data at risk?"

CISO: "We are still investigating. No evidence of exfiltration yet."
CEO: "We do not believe customer data was accessed."
General counsel: "We are assessing whether breach notification is required."

Three different confidence levels. Three different messages. The board immediately questions whether leadership has control.

To prevent misalignment:

- Use consistent language and agree on specific verbs and severity terms.
- Do not contradict each other in front of the board. Resolve differences first.
- Have one spokesperson for each domain: CISO for technical, general counsel for legal, CEO for business impact.

Handling Pressure Questions

During a crisis, board members will ask questions you cannot yet answer, challenge your decisions, or express frustration. You need repeatable techniques for those moments.

Technique 1: Pause and Precision

When you need a moment to think, do not rush. Pause for two to three seconds, then respond with precision.

> **Question:** "How much is this going to cost?"
> **Answer:** "Let me give you the most accurate answer I can right now. Incident response costs are tracking to roughly $75,000 to $150,000 based on forensics and legal. Business impact costs depend on whether we need to take systems offline, which we are assessing now. I will have a more precise estimate by the end of the day once we complete the impact assessment."

The pause signals thoughtfulness, not panic. The answer is clear about what you know and what you do not know.

Technique 2: Validate, Inform, Commit

When asked a question you cannot fully answer yet:

- Validate: acknowledge that the question is important.
- Inform: explain what you know and what you are doing to get the answer.
- Commit: give a specific timeline for when you will have the answer.

Example:

Question: "How did this happen? Why were we not protected?"
Answer: "That is exactly the question we are investigating. Our controls detected and contained the activity, which is why we are having this conversation now. We are conducting a full root cause analysis with external forensics, and I will have preliminary findings for you by 6:00 p.m. tomorrow."

Technique 3: Options and Recommendations

When asked to make a decision or recommendation, lay out options and then recommend one.

Question: "Should we take the affected systems offline?"
Answer: "We have three options. Option 1: Take systems offline immediately. This eliminates risk but disrupts specific operations. Option 2: Isolate systems and monitor. This reduces risk while maintaining operations. Option 3: Continue operations with enhanced monitoring. This maintains business continuity but accepts some residual risk. Based on the current threat assessment, I recommend option 2. It balances risk and business continuity. If the threat escalates, we can move to option 1."

This demonstrates that you have thought through trade-offs and can offer a clear recommendation.

Transitioning from Crisis to Assurance

When containment stabilizes, deliberately shift your language to signal recovery.

- Crisis language (Day 1): "Containment active. Verification in progress. Next update 4:00 p.m."
- Transition language (Day 3): "Containment verified. Impact assessment complete. We are transitioning to the recovery phase."
- Assurance language (Day 7): "Incident closed. Controls restored. After-action review scheduled for the next Audit Committee meeting."

The board hears the progression and reads it as proof of control.

After the Crisis: Rebuilding Confidence

After the crisis is resolved, your relationship with the board enters a critical phase. The technical incident is over, but the governance test continues. How you communicate in the aftermath determines whether the board's confidence in you strengthens or weakens.

What the Board Is Thinking

After a crisis, board members are processing questions like the following:

- Did we get lucky, or are we prepared?
- Will this happen again?

- Can we trust this CISO?
- What do we tell investors, customers, and regulators?

Your after-crisis communication must address these questions directly.

The After-Action Review: What the Board Needs to See

You will typically present an after-action review to the audit committee within two to four weeks of the incident. This is your opportunity to rebuild confidence and demonstrate learning.

Structure your review around three elements: what happened, what worked and what didn't, and what is being improved.

1. What happened (keep this brief)

Provide a concise timeline of key events and decisions, not technical minutiae.

- 2:47 a.m.—Unauthorized access detected
- 3:15 a.m.—Incident response team mobilized
- 3:30 a.m.—CEO and general counsel notified
- 4:00 a.m.—External forensics engaged
- 6:00 a.m.—Containment measures deployed
- 9:00 a.m.—Board chair notified
- Day 2—Forensic analysis complete
- Day 3—Systems restored
- Day 5—Incident closed

Summarize impact: what was and was not affected.

What was affected:

- Supplier gateway environment (isolated, non-production)

- Limited set of customer records accessed (for example, 12,000 records; no evidence of exfiltration)
- Short window of unauthorized database access (for example, 47 minutes)

What was not affected:

- Customer-facing systems (no disruption)
- Production systems (no impact)
- Financial systems (no unauthorized transactions)

Financial impact, for example:

- Incident response costs: $75,000 (forensics, legal, overtime)
- Customer notification costs: $50,000
- Total: $125,000 (within insurance coverage)

2. What worked and what did not

Be honest about both strengths and gaps.

What worked well:

- Detection: SOC identified suspicious activity within minutes.
- Containment: Threat contained within a few hours.
- Communication: Board notified promptly; updates maintained on schedule.
- Coordination: CISO, CEO, and general counsel operated as a unified team.

What took longer than expected:

- Forensic analysis
- Impact assessment

Root cause, for example:

- Compromised supplier credentials were used to access the supplier gateway.
- The supplier did not have multi-factor authentication enabled.
- Third-party access review cycle was quarterly, not continuous.

3. What we are improving

This is the crucial section. The board wants to see that you learned from the incident and are making the program stronger.

Examples of improvements:

- Require MFA for all third-party access.
- Implement near real-time supplier access monitoring.
- Move toward more continuous third-party risk review.
- Enhance detection and monitoring around supplier gateways.
- Refine incident response runbooks based on lessons learned.

For each improvement, specify the owner, timeline, and status. This reads as a strategic assurance review: what changed, why, and how it strengthens the program.

How to Present an After-Action Review Without Being Defensive

Own mistakes directly: "We should have required MFA for supplier access sooner. Here is why we did not, and here is what we have changed."

Frame improvements as program maturation: "This incident revealed gaps in our third-party risk program. We are using it as a catalyst to accelerate improvements we had already prioritized."

Avoid:

- Making excuses: "The supplier should have had better security," even if true, sounds defensive.
- Minimizing: "It was not that bad." The board will assess the level of severity.
- Overpromising: "This will never happen again." No CISO can credibly guarantee that.

End your after-action review with a clear, confident statement:

This incident is closed. We detected the threat quickly, contained it effectively, and learned from it. We have implemented immediate improvements and have a clear plan for longer-term enhancements. Our program is stronger as a result. I am confident in our ability to detect, respond to, and recover from future incidents. Thank you for your support during this event.

This closing signals three things: we are done, we are better, and we are ready.

Norsk Hydro's leadership publicly adopted this approach. After recovering from the attack, executives acknowledged the breach, outlined what they learned, and explained how the company was now better prepared to contain damage more quickly if a similar incident occurred. They did not promise it would never happen again. They showed what they changed and restored confidence.

What to Communicate Versus What to Hold Back

During a crisis, you must balance transparency with operational security, legal privilege, and strategic considerations.

Always communicate the following to the board:

- Confirmed facts about the incident (what, when, where)
- Business impact (operations, customers, revenue, exposure)
- Containment status and your confidence level
- Disclosure obligations and regulatory requirements
- Material matters that require board awareness
- Timeline for resolution and upcoming updates

Communicate the following with caution (coordinate with legal first):

- Attacker identity or attribution (may compromise investigation)
- Specific vulnerabilities exploited (could be used against you)
- Details of ongoing law enforcement engagement
- Preliminary findings that may change

Hold back the following (at least initially):

- Deep technical detail that does not affect business decisions
- Speculation about attacker motives or future actions
- Internal blame or personnel actions (handle separately)
- Information that could compromise the ongoing response

When in doubt, coordinate with general counsel. They can advise what to share, what should be protected by privilege, and how to document board communication appropriately.

What to Carry Forward

- Crisis communication is not about spin or damage control. It is about leadership.
- When a crisis hits, the board is watching to see whether you can do the following:
- See clearly (awareness).
- Act deliberately (control).
- Communicate predictably (discipline).
- If you demonstrate those three signals, the board will trust you to lead through the crisis. If you do not, they will feel obligated to step in.
- Your job is not to make the crisis disappear. Your job is to replace anxiety with structure, randomness with rhythm, and uncertainty with confidence.
- Boards can process bad news. They cannot process unpredictability.
- Your cadence, clarity, and language become the proof that leadership remains in control. Crisis communication is not about resolving the incident. It is about preserving trust while the facts are still moving.

Chapter 11

Aligning Cybersecurity with Business Strategy

Alignment is not an abstract concept. It is a lived experience, often learned through failure. Let me share how I learned this lesson. I learned about strategic alignment the hard way. I remember the first time I built what I thought was a comprehensive security roadmap. It had everything you would expect from a CISO at that point in time. The program was sound, well-documented, and fully aligned with our chosen framework. I was proud of it.

When I presented it at the CEO's staff meeting, I expected questions about timelines or budget. Instead, the CFO asked a simple question: "Which of these initiatives directly supports our expansion into the European market?"

I paused. I had not thought about it that way. My roadmap was built around security maturity, not business strategy. I tried to pivot, explaining how each control would reduce risk across the enterprise. The CFO nodded politely, but I could see I had lost the room. I walked out, realizing I had framed security as overhead rather than enablement.

That moment changed how I approached my role. I stopped building security strategies in isolation. I started with the corporate plan. I worked to convert every security outcome into business language. I began asking executives what kept them up at night, not what controls they thought we needed. Over time, alignment stopped being a presentation tactic and became the foundation of how I led.

This chapter is about that shift. When you align security with business strategy, you stop being a cost center and become a strategic partner.

The board funds what advances objectives, not what slows them. Security strategy only matters when it accelerates business strategy. Your role is not only to protect the company from risk. It is to help leadership decide which risks are worth taking, at what cost, and with what confidence.

Strategy Guardrails

Alignment is not agreement. Alignment ensures the business can pursue its goals without stepping into exposure that undermines the strategy itself.

Most of the time, the answer is a path forward with a trade-off and a timebox. When that happens, do not argue about controls. Reframe the decision in business terms: "This option undermines the objective. Here are two alternatives that preserve speed and confidence."

Guardrails keep security from becoming a veto and keep growth from becoming a gamble.

What Security Strategy Is and Is Not

Security strategy is not a document, a project list, or a catalog of controls. It is the method by which the enterprise decides where security creates business value and how risk is priced into growth. A proper strategy defines choice under constraint.

It answers four questions directors care about:

- Where are we playing? Which markets, data sets, and digital channels matter most to enterprise value, and how can security measure its impact on these areas?
- How are we winning safely? Which capabilities create an advantage while keeping exposure tolerable?
- What are we defending first? Which assets, if compromised, change the earnings call or customer trust, and how do these align with strategic priorities?
- How will we measure confidence? Which indicators prove that protection scales with ambition?

Everything else, including frameworks, roadmaps, and maturity scores, is execution.

The Operator's Definition

Security strategy is the sustained alignment of protection, performance, and trust.

- Protection: The controls that keep the enterprise stable.
- Performance: The speed and efficiency with which the company can act.
- Trust: The confidence investors, regulators, and customers place in that stability.

Your job is to keep those three in balance, never allowing protection to outrun performance or perception to exceed reality.

I saw this balance tested during a major product launch at a previous company. The product team wanted to accelerate the release by six weeks to beat a competitor to market. Engineering was confident they could deliver. The security team, however, identified gaps in the authentication layer that could expose customer data.

The CEO called a meeting. The product lead argued that delaying would cost us market share. The CTO said the code was stable enough. I was the only voice saying we were not ready.

I could have dug in and demanded full remediation before launch. Instead, I reframed the conversation. I acknowledged the business pressure and proposed a middle path: launch on time with compensating controls, including a temporary rate limit and enhanced monitoring. At the same time, we completed the authentication fix in the background. I quantified the residual risk and worked with the general counsel to confirm it was within our acceptable exposure.

The CEO approved the plan. We launched on time, captured market share, and closed the security gap within 30 days. No incidents. No customer impacts.

Was it my first choice? Absolutely not. But we found common ground, and I used the moment to educate the team on the value security can add. That experience reinforced that alignment is not about saying no. It is about finding the path that protects the business while enabling it to move.

Integrating Security into Corporate Objectives

Security alignment starts in the corporate plan. Every enterprise goal, whether it is growth, margin, or trust, carries some level of exposure.

Bridge each goal into a security-enabling statement. If it cannot be translated, it is likely not tied to value. If it is not tied to value, ask yourself why you are doing it.

Examples of translation:

- "Grow subscription revenue in Europe by 20 percent" becomes

"Enable compliant and resilient customer onboarding and data handling in the EU, with exposure within agreed regulatory tolerance."

- "Accelerate cloud migration" becomes "Standardize and automate controls in cloud to enable faster product delivery while preserving trust and uptime."

Once you have tied security outcomes to documented business goals, your next task is to influence how those goals are decided and refined in real time.

Influencing Strategic Decisions

Influence isn't built in the week before a board meeting. It's built over quarters and years through consistent delivery, sound judgment in crises, and a track record of making good calls with imperfect information. Pre-meeting alignment matters, but it only works if you've already earned credibility through execution.

That said, even credible leaders lose budget battles when they fail to prepare the ground. The work before the meeting shapes the outcome in the room.

Brief key executives early. Start with the CEO. For any significant investment, the CEO is your primary sponsor. If the CFO, CTO, and general counsel are aligned but the CEO isn't bought in, you're exposed. Understand the CEO's priorities for the cycle and frame your request against them.

Next, the CFO. CFOs care about financial return, cost avoidance, and risk to margin. Don't pitch product velocity or innovation. Show the math: cost of breach versus cost of control, insurance premium implications, audit findings that carry regulatory penalty risk, or technical debt that compounds operational cost. If you can't make a financial case the CFO finds credible, your proposal isn't ready.

Then the CTO. Be precise. Security controls don't accelerate anything. They enable safe execution and reduce rework from incidents. Frame it honestly: "These controls remove security blockers that are currently slowing migration" or "This reduces the risk of costly rework when we find gaps post-deployment." A sharp CTO will catch overstatement.

Finally, the general counsel. Align on regulatory exposure, disclosure risk, and liability implications. The GC's support strengthens the "cost of inaction" argument.

The Strategic Alignment Cycle

Run this five-step method every quarter. The goal is not to produce more artifacts. It is to keep the security strategy tethered to business intent.

Step 1: Read the Enterprise Plan

Study the corporate strategy, investor letters, and CFO guidance. Highlight the verbs that leadership repeats. Those verbs become your alignment language.

For example, if the verbs are "expand," "optimize," and "simplify," you should be talking about how security expands safely, optimizes operations, and simplifies risk decisions.

Step 2: Map Business Goals to Security Outcomes

Translate each enterprise goal into an enabling security outcome. If you cannot draw a line from the security work to a business goal, question whether it belongs in the plan.

This is where you convert "implement X control" into "enable Y objective by reducing Z exposure."

Step 3: Validate with Business Owners

Review the translations with accountable executives. Ask one direct question: "Does this outcome advance your goal, or slow it down?" Refine until the answer is "advance." If they struggle to see the connection, that is a signal you either need a different framing or a different priority.

Step 4: Reinforce Through Leadership Tone

Between board meetings, reinforce the same alignment language in short executive communications, staff meetings, and strategy reviews.

You are training the organization to hear security as enablement, not noise. Use the same verbs and phrases that appear in the enterprise plan, but now connected to exposure, resilience, and assurance.

Step 5: Review and Reset

End the quarter with a strategic assurance review that addresses the following questions:

- Which trade-offs succeeded?
- Which created friction?
- Which governance gaps remain?

Feed the answers directly into the next planning cycle (shown in Figure 11.1). This is how security alignment becomes a discipline instead of a one-off initiative.

Annual Integration Review

Once a year, consolidate the quarterly outputs into a concise, board-ready strategic assurance report that shows cyber governance as structural, not episodic.

This report should do the following:

- Demonstrate how security supported business strategy over the past 12 months.
- Highlight key decisions influenced, including significant trade-offs and guardrails enforced.
- Summarize measurable outcomes: exposure reduced, resilience improved, and assurance strengthened in the areas that matter most to enterprise value.

You are not just showing activity. You are showing alignment.

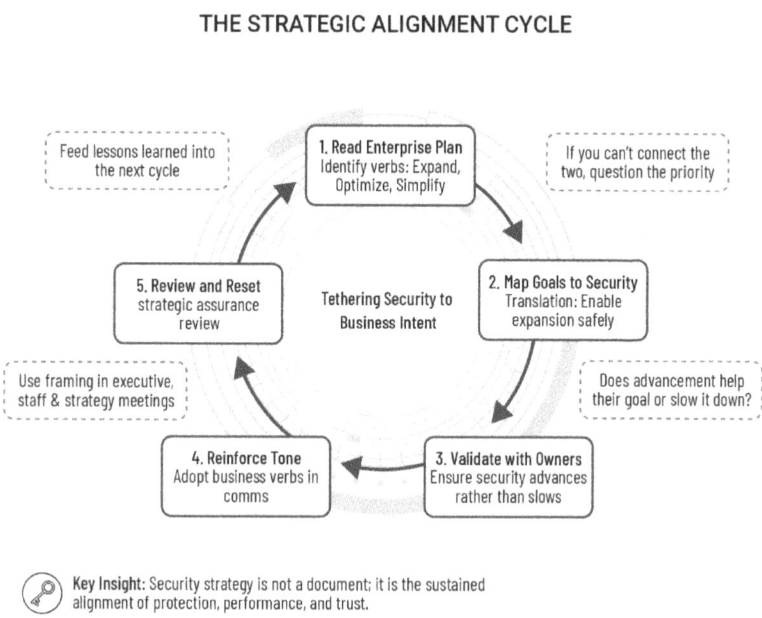

Figure 11.1. The Strategic Alignment Cycle

What to Carry Forward

- Alignment turns cybersecurity from a maturity program into a strategic function. It keeps security tethered to business intent and makes trade-offs explicit:
- What will we protect first?
- What we will be able to do faster?
- What exposure will the company accept to achieve its objectives?
- Influence happens before the meeting, through preparation, shared language, and a united front with the CFO, CTO, and general counsel.
- Treat alignment as a discipline, not a slogan. Read intent, frame choices, reinforce the narrative, and reset through a consistent cycle so security stays positioned as enablement.

Conclusion

Cybersecurity, once a purely technical discipline, has matured into a leadership one. Today, the CISO is not just a guardian of systems but a designer of confidence. The boardroom sees you less as a defender of assets and more as an architect of resilience. That transformation is both a privilege and a challenge. It demands continuous fluency across how the corporation creates value, takes risks, and sustains trust.

If you have reached this page, you have invested time in mastering the most challenging part of leadership: precision under scrutiny. That commitment deserves recognition.

The fact that you are still reading means you have chosen the more challenging road: to keep learning, to keep refining, and to keep showing up with composure when others rush to react. That is what separates competent operators from enduring leaders.

This book is not about security alone. It is about the language of leadership. The boardroom, for all its formality, is human. It rewards those who can bring calm to conflict and order to uncertainty.

The world needs leaders who can turn risk into action and complexity into composure. You are already doing that by reading, reflecting, and deliberately sharpening your skillset.

Keep the conversation going. Share your lessons with peers. Challenge your boards to think in terms of confident outcomes, not compliance checklists. When the room gets tense, when the question feels unfair, or the moment feels rushed, remember the skills you built here.

If this book helped you see the boardroom differently, then it has done its job. Thank you for taking the journey. Now shape the next one.

Acknowledgments

Writing this book has been a privilege, and it would not have been possible without the many executives and board members who allowed me into their conversations over the years. Their candor, questions, and willingness to wrestle with difficult trade-offs shaped much of what you have read.

I am also grateful to the security, technology, and risk leaders who shared their stories, both successes and failures. Many of those moments, anonymized and adapted, became the examples and lessons in these chapters.

To the teams I have had the honor to lead, thank you for your resilience, your curiosity, and your patience with my insistence on precise language. You taught me, every day, that communication is a craft worth practicing.

And finally, thank you, the reader, for investing in your own practice. The real value of this book lies in the conversations you will have and the boards you will influence after you put this book down.

Resources

Board Governance and Oversight

National Association of Corporate Directors (NACD) and Internet Security Alliance, *Director's Handbook on Cyber-Risk Oversight.* Washington, DC: NACD, 2023. Practical guidance for boards on cybersecurity governance and oversight responsibilities.

Information Systems Audit and Control Association (ISACA), *COBIT 2019 Framework: Governance and Management Objectives.* Schaumburg, IL: ISACA, 2019. Establishes governance and management principles for enterprise information systems, including decision rights, accountability, and assurance practices frequently used by regulators and auditors.

Cybersecurity Frameworks and Standards

National Institute of Standards and Technology (NIST), *The NIST Cybersecurity Framework (CSF) 2.0.* Gaithersburg, MD: U.S. Department of Commerce, February 2024. Available at NIST.gov. Comprehensive framework for managing cybersecurity risk across organizations.

International Organization for Standardization and International Electrotechnical Commission, *ISO/IEC 27001:2022: Information Security, Cybersecurity and Privacy Protection—Information Security Management Systems—Requirements.* Geneva: ISO, 2022.

International standard for establishing, implementing, maintaining, and continually improving an information security management system.

Regulatory Requirements

U.S. Securities and Exchange Commission, "Cybersecurity Risk Management, Strategy, Governance, and Incident Disclosure," *Federal Register* 88, no. 159 (August 4, 2023): 51896–51945. Available at SEC.gov. Requires public companies to disclose material cybersecurity incidents and report annually on cybersecurity risk management practices.

European Parliament and Council, Regulation (EU) 2016/679 of the European Parliament and of the Council of 27 April 2016 on the protection of natural persons with regard to the processing of personal data and on the free movement of such data, and repealing Directive 95/46/EC (General Data Protection Regulation). *Official Journal of the European Union* 59, L 119 (May 4, 2016): 1–88. Comprehensive data protection law that establishes requirements for processing personal data of EU residents.

California Legislature, California Consumer Privacy Act (CCPA) of 2018 and California Privacy Rights Act (CPRA) of 2020. California Civil Code §§ 1798.100 et seq. (effective 2020, amended 2023). Establishes consumer privacy rights and business obligations for handling personal information of California residents.

U.S. Department of Health and Human Services, Health Insurance Portability and Accountability Act of 1996 (HIPAA), Public Law 104-191. Washington, DC: HHS, 1996. Establishes national privacy and security standards for protected health information. Non-compliance carries civil and criminal penalties and creates significant trust and reputational consequences for healthcare organizations.

U.S. Congress, Sarbanes-Oxley Act of 2002 (SOX), Public Law 107-204. Washington, DC, 2002. Requires public companies to maintain internal controls over financial reporting, linking cybersecurity control effectiveness to financial integrity, auditability, and accurate disclosures.

Artificial Intelligence Governance

European Parliament and Council, Regulation (EU) 2024/1689 of the European Parliament and of the Council of 13 June 2024 laying down harmonised rules on artificial intelligence amending Regulations (EC) No 300/2008, (EU) No 167/2013, (EU) No 168/2013, (EU) 2018/858, (EU) 2018/1139 and (EU) 2019/2144 and Directives 2014/90/EU, (EU) 2016/797 and (EU) 2020/1828 (Artificial Intelligence Act). *Official Journal of the European Union*, L series, 2024.

See also press releases from the European Council, "Artificial Intelligence Act: Council Gives Final Green Light to the First Worldwide Rules on AI" (May 21, 2024), and from the European Commission, "AI Act Enters Into Force" (August 1, 2024).

National Institute of Standards and Technology (NIST), *Artificial Intelligence Risk Management Framework (AI RMF 1.0)*. Gaithersburg, MD: U.S. Department of Commerce, January 2023; updated as *NIST AI RMF Playbook* and supplementary guidance, 2024. Available at NIST.gov. Framework for managing risks associated with artificial intelligence systems.

Organisation for Economic Co-operation and Development (OECD), "OECD Framework for the Classification of AI Systems." *OECD Digital Economy Papers* No. 323. Paris: OECD Publishing, 2022. See also OECD AI Principles (2019), adopted by 46 countries. Establishes a common taxonomy and principles for responsible AI development.

Implementation Standards

Center for Internet Security (CIS), CIS Critical Security Controls

Version 8. East Greenbush, NY: CIS, 2021. https://www.cisecurity.org/controls/v8. Provides a prioritized and prescriptive set of cybersecurity controls that serve as an implementation layer guiding foundational security investments and measurable risk reduction.

U.S. Department of Defense, Cybersecurity Maturity Model Certification (CMMC) Program. Office of the Chief Information Officer, updated 2024. Establishes a tiered cybersecurity maturity framework and assessment requirements for defense industrial base contractors that handle Federal Contract Information (FCI) and Controlled Unclassified Information (CUI). Non-compliance can result in loss of contract eligibility and direct revenue impact for organizations in the defense industrial base.

Contractual Mandates

Payment Card Industry Security Standards Council, Payment Card Industry Data Security Standard (PCI DSS), Version 4.0. PCI DSS: v4.0.1. Wakefield, MA: PCI SSC, 2022. Defines mandatory security requirements for organizations that store, process, or transmit cardholder data. Enforcement is contractual through payment brands and acquiring banks, and non-compliance risks loss of payment processing capability.

Risk Quantification Frameworks

The Open Group, *The Open Group Standard for Risk Taxonomy (O-RT)*, Version 3.0.1, and *The Open Group Standard for Risk Analysis (O-RA)*, Version 2.0.1. San Francisco: The Open Group, 2021. Provides a taxonomy and methodology for quantifying information risk in financial terms, enabling consistent measurement and comparison of cyber risk across an organization.

Appendix A

Glossary of Boardroom Terms with CISO Translations

Assurance

Board Definition: Independent validation that controls, processes, and risk management activities are working as intended.

CISO Translation: Boards expect more than claims of security. They want evidence. Dashboards, audits, tests, and metrics create assurance about exposure and resilience.

Context: Use when explaining why audits, red team exercises, or third-party reviews are needed.

Assurance Level

Board Definition: The degree of confidence the board can reasonably place in the information and conclusions being presented.

CISO Translation: It is not enough to show numbers. You must explain how validated they are and where uncertainty remains.

Context: Use when describing how data is verified, cross-checked, or supported by independent review.

Board Culture

Board Definition: The norms, habits, and unwritten rules that shape how directors discuss issues and exercise oversight.

CISO Translation: How you frame risk must match how the board operates, whether formal or informal, skeptical or supportive, analytical or narrative.

Context: Use when coaching your team or external advisors on how to show up in front of this specific board.

Board Governance

Board Definition: The system of processes, structures, and decision rights through which the board directs and oversees the organization.

CISO Translation: The board expects cyber risk to be integrated into its governance rhythm, with regular reporting, clear ownership, and measurable assurance.

Context: Use when proposing reporting cadences or explaining where cybersecurity fits within board oversight.

Disclosure Risk

Board Definition: The risk that a cyber, privacy, or AI issue triggers mandatory reporting to regulators, customers, or investors, and the consequences of getting that disclosure wrong.

CISO Translation: The danger is not just the incident itself, but failing to disclose it accurately, on time, and in a way that withstands scrutiny.

Context: Use when discussing SEC rules, breach notification laws, or the reputational impact of public statements.

Duty of Loyalty

Board Definition: A director's obligation to act in the best interests of the organization and its shareholders, free from conflicts of interest.

CISO Translation: Directors expect you to disclose risks fully, avoid selective framing, and present options that reflect the organization's best interests, not departmental bias.

Context: Use when aligning cybersecurity recommendations to enterprise priorities, not just security preferences.

Duty of Oversight (Caremark Duty)

Board Definition: A director's responsibility to ensure systems exist to detect, escalate, and manage risk, including cyber.

CISO Translation: The board relies on you to demonstrate that the organization has governance structures, controls, and monitoring in place for cyber risk, and that this feeds into their view of exposure and assurance.

Context: Use when explaining risk dashboards, governance committees, or why specific reporting mechanisms must be formalized.

Enterprise Risk Management (ERM)

Board Definition: A holistic approach to identifying, evaluating, and managing the organization's top risks across all functions.

CISO Translation: Cybersecurity must be framed as an enterprise risk, not a technical one. Your updates should integrate into the same structure and priority tier as financial, operational, and strategic risks.

Context: Use when presenting top cyber risks, risk appetite, or integration with corporate risk registers.

Escalation Path

Board Definition: The defined route by which issues move from staff to management to committees and, if necessary, to the full board.

CISO Translation: You need a clear map of who gets told what and when, so no one is surprised when a risk crosses a threshold.

Context: Use when describing governance workflows or preparing for how cyber incidents will be communicated.

Executive Session

Board Definition: A closed portion of a meeting where directors may meet alone or with selected executives, without the full management team present.

CISO Translation: Being invited into an executive session signals deeper trust, or significant concern. In that room, brevity and candor matter more than slides.

Context: Use when preparing for sensitive discussions such as major incidents, systemic risk, or leadership performance.

Loss Event

Board Definition: An incident that results in measurable financial, operational, legal, or reputational impact.

CISO Translation: Not every alert or breach is a loss event. It becomes one when there is real, quantifiable damage.

Context: Use when differentiating noise, incidents, and events that affect earnings, customers, or public trust.

Materiality

Board Definition: Whether a cyber incident or risk is significant enough that a reasonable investor would consider it essential.

CISO Translation: You must frame impact in business terms, such as operations, customers, revenue, or valuation, not technical terms.

Context: Use during incident briefings or when assessing whether a breach must be escalated to the board and disclosed.

Operational Resilience

Board Definition: The organization's ability to continue delivering critical services during and after disruptions.

CISO Translation: Cyber goes beyond security. It is core to keeping the business running. The board expects you to explain resilience in terms of operations and customers.

Context: Use during discussions of continuity, ransomware, or overall crisis posture.

Oversight Threshold

Board Definition: The point at which a risk, incident, or trend becomes significant enough that the board must be informed or involved.

CISO Translation: The line where an issue stops being a management-only topic and must be escalated with framing and options for directors.

Context: Use when defining which cyber, privacy, or AI issues will be brought to the board or committee and why.

Reputational Harm

Board Definition: Damage to trust, brand, or stakeholder confidence that influences customer behavior, valuation, or strategic opportunities.

CISO Translation: The board often cares more about how an event looks and feels externally than how it occurred technically.

Context: Use when explaining why some incidents require a rapid, visible response, even if the technical impact is limited.

Residual Risk

Board Definition: The risk remaining after all controls, mitigations, and safeguards are applied.

CISO Translation: No matter how strong controls are, some risk always remains. You must articulate whether that residual exposure is acceptable.

Context: Use during roadmap discussions or when explaining why additional investment is still needed.

Risk Appetite

Board Definition: The level of risk the board is willing to accept in pursuit of its strategic objectives.

CISO Translation: Your job is to show whether the current cyber risk is above, within, or below board-approved tolerance, and what actions or authorizations are needed to bring it back within tolerance.

Context: Use when translating threat data into directional posture or when making investment requests.

Risk Register

Board Definition: A documented inventory of the organization's top risks, their likelihood, impact, and mitigation status.

CISO Translation: Your top cyber risks must appear in this register in board-level language. If not, the board may assume cyber is not a priority risk.

Context: Use when connecting cybersecurity to enterprise risk reporting.

Risk Tolerance

Board Definition: The specific boundaries of risk variation that the organization can withstand before action must be taken.

CISO Translation: Helps you frame cyber metrics as thresholds that trigger action, for example, "If detection falls below X, we escalate."

Context: Use when presenting key risk indicators, thresholds, or escalation triggers.

Risk Transfer

Board Definition: Shifting financial risk to a third party, such as through insurance or contract terms.

CISO Translation: Helps frame cyber insurance as a strategic financial mitigation, not a substitute for controls.

Context: Use when explaining the limits of insurance and why risk cannot be fully transferred.

Scenario Analysis

Board Definition: The practice of evaluating realistic "what if" situations to understand potential impacts and response options.

CISO Translation: Boards use scenarios to test whether the organization is prepared, not to hear every technical detail.

Context: Use when discussing tabletop exercises, AI failure scenarios, or supply chain attacks in board language.

Strategic Alignment

Board Definition: The degree to which an initiative, investment, or risk decision supports the organization's long-term strategy.

CISO Translation: Cyber, data, and AI decisions must be framed as helping or hindering growth, innovation, and competitive position.

Context: Use when justifying major security or trust investments, or when explaining why a "no" is a protective strategy.

Strategic Risk

Board Definition: Risks that could materially impact long-term strategy, competitive advantage, or market position.

CISO Translation: Show how cyber threats affect product launches, acquisitions, expansion, innovation, or valuation.

Context: Use when you want the board to understand cyber as a business inhibitor or enabler, not just a technical function.

Appendix B

Board Meeting Checklist

Preparing for Your Next Board Meeting

This checklist guides CISOs through a systematic approach to preparing for board presentations and committee briefings. Use it to ensure clarity, alignment, and confidence in every board engagement.

Four Weeks Before the Meeting

Understand the Board's Current State of Mind

- Review previous meeting minutes. What cybersecurity topics were discussed? What questions or concerns were raised?
- Identify recent events affecting the board. Has there been a breach in your industry, regulatory changes, investor pressure, or executive turnover?
- Check the board agenda. What other topics are being discussed? How does cybersecurity fit into the broader agenda?

Clarify Objectives and Desired Outcomes

- Define your goal: What do you want the board to know?
- Awareness: Inform the board of trends, threats, or initiatives.

- Approval: Seek approval for budget, strategy, or policy change.
- Assurance: Demonstrate control effectiveness and program maturity.
- Escalation: Alert the board to elevated risk or an incident.
- Draft a one-sentence objective. For example: "The board will approve a $2M investment in zero trust architecture to reduce lateral movement risk by 60 percent within 18 months."
- Identify success metrics. How will you know the presentation was effective?

Coordinate with Stakeholders

- Align with the CEO. Brief the CEO on your board message, ensure no surprises, and confirm executive support.
- Coordinate with the CFO. Validate financial data, budget requests, and ROI claims.
- Engage general counsel. Review legal, regulatory, and disclosure implications, especially for incidents or material risks.
- Consult with the board or committee chair. Understand the chair's priorities and any sensitivities.
- Brief other C-suite leaders. Ensure leaders are aware of your message, especially if it is cross-functional.

Two to Three Weeks Before the Meeting

Develop Core Content

- Draft your executive summary, ideally one page. Focus on what, why it matters, options, recommendations, and action required. Use the one-page executive summary pattern from the main text.
- Prepare supporting materials as needed, such as a quarterly dashboard for routine updates or an incident brief if escalating an event.
- Translate technical concepts into business language. Replace jargon with impact-focused terms.

- Quantify where possible. Use financial impact, risk reduction percentages, or time to value estimates.
- Frame risks in terms of board priorities: risk, value, reputation, compliance, and strategy.

Build Visuals and Dashboards

- Create board-friendly visuals.
- Include trend lines, such as improving, stable, or declining.
- Simplify charts. Aim for one primary message per visual.
- Limit text on slides. Use headlines and key data only.
- Design for tablet readability. Many directors review materials on mobile devices while traveling.
- Test visual clarity. Can someone unfamiliar with cybersecurity understand your charts in ten seconds?

Anticipate Questions

- List the most likely board questions. For example: "How does this compare to our peers?" "What is the worst-case scenario?" "Why now?" "What happens if we do nothing?" "How confident are you in this recommendation?"
- Prepare concise, confident answers. Practice delivering each answer in 30 to 60 seconds.
- Prepare for "What do you not know?" questions. Acknowledge uncertainty transparently and explain how you are addressing unknowns.
- Identify potential director hot buttons. Which directors have been vocal on security topics, and what are their concerns?

One Week Before the Meeting

Submit Pre-Read Materials

Finalize all materials, including the executive summary, dashboards, and appendices.

- Have materials reviewed by the CEO.
- Have materials reviewed by general counsel for legal and regulatory accuracy.
- Have materials reviewed by the CFO for financial accuracy.
- If public disclosure may be involved, have materials reviewed by communications or investor relations.
- Submit materials to the board secretary. Meet the deadline for inclusion in the board packet, typically five to seven days before the meeting.

Conduct Internal Dry Run

- Present to a peer or mentor. Practice your delivery and get feedback.
- Role-play difficult questions. Have someone challenge you with skeptical or unexpected questions.
- Time your presentation. Ensure you can deliver key messages within the allocated time, typically five to ten minutes.
- Refine based on feedback. Adjust messaging, visuals, or flow as needed.

Coordinate Logistics

- Confirm your time slot. Know when you present, how long you have, and whether questions will be taken during or after your remarks.
- Verify technology setup. Will you present remotely or in person? Are there screen-sharing or connectivity requirements?
- Prepare backup materials. Have printed copies in case of technical issues.
- Coordinate with other presenters. If you are presenting with the CFO, CTO, or general counsel, align on who will cover which topics.

One to Two Days Before the Meeting

Final Review and Mental Preparation

- Review the whole board packet, if possible. Understand how your topic fits within the broader agenda.
- Re-read your materials. Ensure you can speak fluently about every chart, claim, and recommendation.
- Refresh on your answers to anticipated questions. Practice delivering concise, confident responses.
- Prepare your opening statement. Craft a strong, 30-second framing that sets the tone.
- Get a good night's sleep. Mental clarity and composure are your greatest assets.

Day of the Meeting

Pre-Meeting Preparation, Morning

- Review key talking points. Focus on your core message and recommendation.
- Check email for last-minute updates. Has anything changed that affects your presentation?
- Test technology. If presenting remotely, confirm connectivity, audio, and screen sharing.
- Arrive early if you are in person. Set up, test equipment, and settle in.
- Breathe and center yourself. Confidence comes from preparation and composure.

During Your Presentation

- Read the room. Observe body language, engagement, and reactions. Adjust tone or pace if needed.
- Lead with the "so what." Start with impact, not background.

- Stick to your time limit. Respect the board's agenda.
- Pause after key points. Let the message land and invite questions.
- Answer questions directly. If you do not know, say so and commit to follow-up timing.
- Close with clarity. Restate the action requested and next steps.

Immediately After Your Presentation

- Thank the board. A brief acknowledgment shows professionalism.
- Note questions or concerns raised. Capture follow-up items while they are fresh.
- Debrief with the CEO or general counsel, if available. Do a quick check-in on how it went and any immediate actions.

Within 24 to 48 Hours After the Meeting

Follow-Up and Documentation

- Send follow-up materials. Answer any questions that required research or additional detail.
- Document commitments made. What did you promise to deliver, and by when?
- Update stakeholders. Brief your team, CFO, CTO, and general counsel on outcomes and next steps.
- Reflect on performance. What went well, and what would you do differently next time?

Within One Week After the Meeting

Execution and Accountability

- Set up tracking for board commitments. Create internal milestones to ensure timely delivery.
- Schedule the next board update. Confirm timing and format for the next touchpoint.

- Incorporate board feedback into future presentations. Commit to continuous improvement in your communication approach.

Quarterly or Annual Review

- Review all board interactions over the past quarter or year. Identify patterns, recurring questions, and areas for improvement.
- Solicit feedback from the board chair or committee chair. Ask for candid input on your communication effectiveness.
- Update your board communication playbook. Refine templates, talking points, and materials based on what works.
- Benchmark against peers. Compare your board reporting approach with industry practices you respect.

Quick Reference: The Night-Before Checklist

Use this condensed checklist for a final review the evening before your board presentation.

- I can state my objective in one sentence.
- I have reviewed all submitted materials and can speak fluently about them.
- I have prepared concise answers to the top ten likely questions.
- I have aligned with the CEO, CFO, and general counsel.
- I know my time slot, format, and technology requirements.
- I have a strong opening and a clear closing statement.
- I am mentally prepared and confident in my approach.

Remember: Preparation reduces anxiety and increases credibility. The board trusts leaders who demonstrate discipline, clarity, and command of their domain. This checklist helps you show up prepared, confident, and ready to lead.

Appendix C

The Boardroom Operating System (OS)

This "operating system" is a repeatable framework for every board interaction. Use it to ensure you are showing up, framing issues, and moving the business forward with the consistency the boardroom demands.

The Core Principles

Start With Business Outcomes

Before any board meeting, ask yourself:

- What are the top three business outcomes the board cares about right now (e.g., growth, margin, customer trust, regulatory scrutiny)?
- How does security help protect or enable each of those outcomes?
- What's the key takeaway I want them to leave with?

Frame Issues as Risk, Time, and Trade-Offs

The board's mental model is risk, not technology. Discipline yourself to answer three things for every issue:

Impact

If this risk materializes, what happens to revenue, operations, or reputation?

Example: "If our payment gateway goes down, we lose $400K per hour in transactions and trigger service-level penalties with our largest customers."

Likelihood and time horizon

Is this a near-term issue or an emerging strategic pressure?

Example: "This vulnerability is actively being exploited in our sector—three competitors were hit in the last 60 days, so the likelihood is high and immediate."

Trade-offs

What do we gain and what do we give up with each option (e.g., speed vs. control)?

Example: "We can launch in 30 days with basic controls, or wait 60 days for full security hardening. A faster launch means accepting elevated risk for the first quarter."

Pre-Align, Then Perform

The real work happens before the meeting starts:

- Socialize your message early, especially any hard news, with the leadership team to ensure you all speak with one voice.
- Ensure there are no surprises when you are "on stage."

Boardroom OS: Pre-Flight Checklist

Use this checklist as a final self-check before your next board interaction:

- I can name the top three business outcomes the board cares about this quarter.

- Every topic I plan to raise is tied to at least one of those outcomes.
- For each significant risk, I can state impact, likelihood, and trade-offs in business terms.
- My metrics are consistent with prior meetings and tied to outcomes, not just activity.
- I have pre-briefed the CEO and relevant directors on sensitive items or significant asks.
- I can state, in one sentence, the narrative of our security journey since the last meeting.

Appendix D

Board Question Bank

This appendix consolidates the board questions and recommended answers from throughout the book, organized by the scenario you are preparing for. The source chapter and section are noted for each answer for cross-reference.

Framework and Governance Questions

Use these to prepare for board questions on your cybersecurity framework strategy, framework adoption, or governance maturity. These questions typically arise during routine quarterly updates or when the board is evaluating framework investments. You can find these in Chapter 5, Common Board Questions About Frameworks (and How to Answer Them).

"Which framework should we use?"

> "It depends on three factors: regulatory requirements, customer expectations, and our maturity level. Most organizations use a combination. For us, I recommend [frameworks] because [business rationale: regulatory alignment, customer needs, practical implementation]. As we mature, we can add [additional frameworks] to close specific gaps."

"How much will this cost?"

"Framework adoption has three cost components: initial assessment, implementation, and ongoing maintenance. For this program, we expect an initial investment of approximately [X] over [Y] months. The return comes from lower regulatory risk, potential reductions in cyber insurance premiums, and faster customer or M&A due diligence. We will report progress and ROI using clear metrics."

"Are we compliant with this framework?"

"Compliance is not binary; it is a maturity journey. Today we are at [current state], with roughly [percentage] of key controls implemented. Our target is [future state] by [date], aligned to [business goal]. We will report progress quarterly using maturity and performance metrics tied to business outcomes."

"Do our competitors use this framework?"

"Most organizations in our sector use some combination of NIST, ISO, COBIT, and CIS. These have become expectations in regulatory reviews, customer assessments, and requests for proposals. Not aligning to them would put us at a disadvantage in areas such as regulatory standing and customer trust."

"How do we know it is working?"

"We measure effectiveness through three lenses: independent audits (external validation), control testing results (internal assurance), and incident response performance (real-world outcomes). We will report those results regularly so you can see how framework adoption improves over time."

"Can we get certified?"

"ISO 27001 offers formal certification, which many customers require. NIST and COBIT do not provide certification in the same way, but we can benchmark our maturity against them. ISO 27001 certification typically takes eight months and costs approximately $175k. The business value is better customer access, stronger regulatory posture, and a clearer story for investors and partners."

Regulatory and Compliance Questions

Use these to prepare for board questions about regulatory posture, compliance status, or adaptation to new laws. These questions typically arise when regulatory changes are in the news, during audit committee briefings, or when entering new markets. You can find these in Chapter 6, Common Board Questions About Compliance (and How to Answer Them).

"Are we compliant?"

"We are compliant with current requirements in [list key regulations]. We have a structured process to monitor new obligations and absorb them within 90 days. Our last external audit confirmed no material gaps."

"What happens if we are not compliant?"

"Non-compliance with GDPR could result in fines of up to four percent of global revenue, but the larger risk is reputational. Customers and partners expect us to protect their data. Non-compliance with SEC disclosure rules could trigger investor lawsuits and analyst downgrades. Non-compliance with the Payment Card Industry Data Security Standard, PCI-DSS, could mean we lose the ability to process credit card payments."

"How fast can we adapt when regulations change?"

"Our regulatory monitoring process flags new obligations within 30 days of passage. We assess impact within 60 days and implement required controls within 90 days. We track this as 'change velocity,' and we report it quarterly so you can see our adaptation tempo."

"What is our exposure in [specific geography or industry]?"

"For the EU, we are aligned with GDPR, and based on our business in California, we are aligned with CCPA and monitoring pending amendments. We have gap assessments underway for [state or region], and we will brief the board on any material exposure next quarter."

AI and Emerging Technology Questions

Use these to prepare for board questions on AI governance, AI risk, or the controls around AI-driven business decisions. These questions are increasingly common as organizations deploy AI in revenue and customer-facing systems. You can find these in Chapter 7, Common Board Questions About AI (and How to Answer Them).

"How do we know our AI isn't biased?"

"We test for disparate impact before deployment and monitor outcomes by demographic group. Our 1.8% appeal rate tells us customers trust the system is fair."

"What happens if AI makes a decision that causes significant financial harm?"

"Our pricing AI has three protection layers: 15% adjustment limit, daily VP review with override authority, and real-time anomaly alerts. Worst case, we revert to manual pricing within hours."

"Isn't AI just a black box we can't control?"

"For high-stakes decisions like credit, we use explainable models.

For lower-risk systems, we focus on governing outcomes—monitoring fairness, enabling overrides, and detecting problems quickly."

"How much is this costing us?"

"AI governance costs about 8% of our total AI investment, roughly $400K annually. One regulatory penalty for bias could easily be double that number."

"Do we need a separate AI committee, or can this stay with the Audit Committee?"

"AI oversight can stay with audit or risk if they have the bandwidth. What matters is that someone at the board level asks the three governance questions regularly: What decisions is AI making? Who's accountable? How do we know it's working?"

Post-Incident and Crisis Questions

Use these when you are briefing the board during or after a cybersecurity incident. These questions test your composure, your command of the facts, and your ability to demonstrate control under pressure.

"Was customer data exposed in the incident?"

Answer: "No. We confirmed that no data left the environment."
Assurance: "We validated this through log review and third-party forensics within 12 hours of detection."
Next step: "The full forensics report is in the appendix, and I can walk you through the methodology after the meeting if helpful."

Source: Chapter 9, Handling Q&A and Difficult Conversations

"So what you are saying is we are vulnerable."

"What I am saying is we have residual risk in this area, which is within our stated risk appetite. We are actively managing it through compensating controls and targeted investments. The trajectory is toward lower exposure, and we will report progress quarterly."

Source: Chapter 9, When a Director Challenges Your Framing

"Why were we not told about this sooner?"

"We notified the audit chair within 24 hours of confirming the issue met our materiality threshold. I agree that timeliness is critical, which is why we have strengthened our escalation criteria to surface issues earlier in the assessment process. The updated framework went into effect last month, and we will report on its effectiveness at the next meeting."

Source: Chapter 9, Ambush Questions

"How did this happen?"

"Root cause analysis is underway. Current evidence points to compromised supplier credentials. We will have confirmed findings in our after-action review by [date]."

Source: Chapter 10, Before and After Examples

"Are we going to be in the news?"

"Based on current evidence, no customer data is compromised, there is no operational disruption, and no regulatory notification is required. I do not expect this to become public. However, we are coordinating with communications and legal to prepare for any scenario. If that assessment changes, I will notify you immediately."

Source: Chapter 10, Before and After Examples

"Could this happen again?"

"We are implementing immediate containment measures and will conduct a full control review. Systemic improvements will be prioritized in our after-action plan. I will present specific enhancements to the audit committee within 30 days."

Source: Chapter 10, Before and After Examples

"How much is this going to cost?"

"Let me give you the most accurate answer I can right now. Incident response costs are tracking to roughly $75,000 to $150,000 based on forensics and legal. Business impact costs depend on whether we need to take systems offline, which we are assessing now. I will have a more precise estimate by the end of the day once we complete the impact assessment."

Source: Chapter 10, Handling Pressure Questions

"How did this happen? Why were we not protected?"

"That is exactly the question we are investigating. Our controls detected and contained the activity, which is why we are having this conversation now. We are conducting a full root cause analysis with external forensics, and I will have preliminary findings for you by 6:00 p.m. tomorrow."

Source: Chapter 10, Handling Pressure Questions

"Should we take the affected systems offline?"

"We have three options. Option 1: Take systems offline immediately. This eliminates risk but disrupts specific operations. Option 2: Isolate systems and monitor. This reduces risk while maintaining operations. Option 3: Continue operations with enhanced monitoring. This maintains business continuity but accepts some residual risk. Based on the current threat assessment, I recommend option 2. It balances risk and business continuity. If the threat escalates, we can move to option 1."

Source: Chapter 10, Handling Pressure Questions

Budget and Investment Questions

Use these to prepare for board questions about the financial justification for security investments, the cost of risk, or return on security spending. These questions arise during budget approval cycles or when you are requesting new investment.

"What's the dollar amount?" / "What's our exposure in dollars?" / "What's the ROI on this security investment?"

Work with the CFO; don't quantify in isolation. Financial risk quantification is the CFO's domain. When boards ask for dollar amounts, this is your opportunity to demonstrate executive alignment, not technical expertise.

Use ranges, not point estimates. Say "$4 to 4.5 million potential exposure" rather than "$4.3 million." Ranges acknowledge uncertainty while still providing context.

Use scenarios rather than predictions. "If ransomware takes down our core systems, recovery costs $X to $Y based on downtime duration. Here's our current recovery capability."

Focus on relative priority. "This risk is higher than that risk because..." Boards need to know where to allocate resources, not exact dollar precision.

Be transparent about uncertainty. When boards press for precision you cannot provide, explain why: "The honest answer is that we cannot quantify this with confidence. Here's what we know, here's what we don't know, and here's how we're managing the uncertainty."

Source: Chapter 8, When Boards Ask: "What's the Dollar Amount?"

www.ingramcontent.com/pod-product-compliance
Lightning Source LLC
LaVergne TN
LVHW051058210926
848486LV00024B/419/J
9798994643501